Bene Appétit

The Cuisine of Indian Jews

Esther David

HarperCollins *Publishers* India

First published in India by
HarperCollins *Publishers* in 2021
Building 10, Tower A, 4th Floor, DLF Cyber City, Phase II,
Gurugram Haryana – 122002, India
www.harpercollins.co.in

2 4 6 8 10 9 7 5 3 1

P-ISBN: 978-93-5357-957-9
E-ISBN: 978-93-5357-958-6

Typeset in 11/15.2 Linux Libertine at
Manipal Technologies Limited, Manipal

Printed and bound at
MicroPrints India, New Delhi

Bene Appétit

Also by the author

Bombay Brides

L'Chaim...
To Life...

Contents

Prologue

This book is like a journey. In the course of writing it, I travelled to the seven main centres where Indian Jews live, in different Indian cities and states. I discovered how Indian Jews have preserved their food habits in a multicultural country like India, which has diverse cuisines. Indian Jews follow a strict dietary law of kosher but have derived ways and means of using the correct regional ingredients to abide by this law. This journey was an eye-opener for me, as it brought to light that each community has a different culinary method, which is influenced by regional Indian cooking.

There are about five thousand Jews and five Jewish communities in India, but they are fast diminishing in number. Till 1940 there were about 50,000 Jews in India. But soon after the independence of Israel, during the 1950s, many Jewish families emigrated back there and to other Western countries. They often return to India, and are seen in the synagogues of Mumbai, Pune, Ahmedabad and Alibaug during weddings, bar mitzvahs and Yom Kippur.

I had planned this journey to discover the food traditions of these communities. Traditional Indian Jewish food is a dying art.

The Bene Israel Jewish community is the largest in India. They live in western India – in Mumbai and its environs, as well as in Alibaug and its surroundings in Raigad district, Maharashtra; and in Ahmedabad, Vadodara, Rajkot, Rajpipla and Palanpur in Gujarat.

Then there are the Cochin Jews in Kochi and its environs in Kerala; the Baghdadi Jews in Kolkata, West Bengal; the Bene Ephraim Jews in Vijayawada and its environs and in Machilipatnam, Andhra Pradesh. In the Northeast, we have the Bnei Menashe Jews in Aizawl, Mizoram, and in Imphal and Churachandpur, Manipur.

All these communities have different ways of following the dietary law in their food habits, yet there is a common thread, which links each community to the other.

The strict dietary law referred to above is of not mixing dairy products with meat dishes. Indian Jews also have fish with scales. Pork is taboo. They prefer to end their meals with fruit or betel leaf and betel nut. And, as a substitute to dairy products, they use coconut milk to make curries, sweets and other recipes.

Indian Jews have thorough knowledge about the animals they can and cannot eat. There is always a Jewish elder, known as shohet, in each community, who knows the law of kosher to slaughter animals. As kosher meat is not easily available in India, a majority of Indian Jews are vegetarians and have a variety of dairy-based foods with their meals.

Most Jewish communities live around seashores, lakes and rivers and have a preference for fish and rice. Many of the members took to the urban way of life and moved to cities; before that they were farmers who owned paddy fields, along with coconut and banana plantations. The Bene Israel Jews were known to be oilpressers.

During this journey, I had to deal with the languages spoken in various regions – Telugu in Andhra Pradesh, Malayalam in Kochi, Bengali in Kolkata, Mizo and Manipuri in northeast India and Marathi in western India. I had to find interpreters in almost all areas, as I can only speak English, Hindi and Gujarati. It is important to mention that while most Indian Jews speak English, along with the regional languages, they say their prayers in Hebrew.

My first stop was Machilipatnam, where there was a small synagogue, to meet the Bene Ephraim Jews of Andhra Pradesh. I had read about this community earlier. In 2010, I had seen a short film about the Bene Ephraim Community Synagogue of Machilipatnam, and was fascinated by it. Later, Anjali K., a student from CEPT University, Ahmedabad, visited this synagogue and sent me the email address of Dr Mukthipudi Jaya Kumar Jacob, fondly known as Jaya Kumar. Before leaving for Andhra Pradesh, I had sent a questionnaire to Jaya Kumar, which he had translated into Telugu and passed on to his community members to send him the necessary information about their cuisine. He had then translated their inputs into English and sent me detailed information.

My next stop was Kerala. Cochin Jews are very few in number. In 2004, when I was in Kochi as a jury member for the forty-sixth national exhibition of art, I had met Elias Joseph Hai and his wife Ofera at the Kadavumbagam Synagogue, which was under repair at the time. Elias has a shop of tropical fish, aquariums and exotic plants in the foyer of the synagogue.

In 2017, the Kadavumbagam Synagogue was renovated by Elias Joseph Hai. It was ready for services, but did not have a Torah

Scroll, also known as the Sefer Torah, a book of Hebrew religious literature, which is handwritten with a quill on specially prepared parchment, rolled into a scroll, placed in a casket and installed in an ark or cupboard at the synagogue. Reading a Torah Scroll is the religious law, which is known as Halakha. The word 'Torah' literally means teachings of the Five Books of Moses, which are at the core of Jewish history and law.

The trustees of the synagogue received a Torah in 2018 as a gift from Israel and since then religious services have been held there.

Before flying to Kochi for my book, I had called Ofera from Ahmedabad. She recognized me and we decided to meet at the newly renovated Kadavumbagam Synagogue. After I landed at the Cochin International Airport and went to the synagogue, Ofera was waiting for me. We sat on a bench in a quiet corner of her shop and I told her about my project. She agreed to send me details about the traditional food of Cochin Jews. On my return to Ahmedabad, a month later, I received an email from Ofera with information about the Cochin Jewish community and their recipes.

For Aizawl and Imphal, I had received some contact numbers from an Ahmedabad-based professor at the Indian Institute of Management, Anil K. Gupta. Earlier, at a literature conference in Israel in 2017, I had also met Dr Margaret Ch. Zama from Aizawl. She had given me some invaluable information about northeast India. I received Yonathan Lallawmsanga's mobile number from Dr Zama's friend Ms Zaithanchhungi, a well-known writer and researcher on the Jew–Mizo connection. Yonathan was helpful and even sent the necessary papers for me to get military permission to enter Mizoram. But when I was in Aizawl, I could not manage to meet him. Only on my last day in Aizawl did Yonathan and his mother Tamar come to meet me at the restaurant of the hotel where I was staying. I took notes and also gave them questionnaires to collect information about their cuisine. Two months later, Yonathan sent me details about their cuisine, as well as recipes and photographs.

It was easier to collect information about the Bnei Menashe Jewish community of Manipur, as I had been given the phone number of Lhingneikim Manchong by my Israeli friends Myriam Damoni and Esther Thangjom Schomberg. Lhingneikim methodically answered all my questions in English and sent me details of food, recipes and photographs. But by the time I could go to Imphal, she had moved to Guwahati in Assam. Still, she sent me the contact numbers of Meital Singson and Akiva Haokip Khailen of the Shevei Israel Group of Imphal.

Manipur has a small community of Jews. I called Akiva and he came to meet me and gave me the details I needed, while I made notes and gave him a questionnaire. On my return to Ahmedabad, I received more information from Akiva about the Bnei Menashe cuisine, as well as some photographs.

In Kolkata, I met Ian Zachariah, a well-known name in journalism and advertising who is also an authority on Baghdadi Jewish food. He has been sending me details about his community for the last few years. He gave me invaluable insight into the Baghdadi Jewish cuisine. I gave him the questionnaire, which he sent back with detailed answers as well as an article he had written about Baghdadi Jewish cuisine and some recipes, which he had collected from relatives living in London. I also visited a Jewish bakery, where they had specially baked challah bread for me, which is traditionally made for Shabbath.

I live in western India and have studied the Bene Israel Jewish cuisine for many years. Through the years, I have written novels based on the Jewish experience of living in India. During this period, Julie Joseph Pingle gave me detailed information about Bene Israel Jewish food and even made some recipes for me. Her husband,

Joseph Samuel Pingle, is the hazzan or cantor of the synagogue in Ahmedabad.

Looking back, I noticed that the Jews of these five regions have different facial characteristics. When I photographed them, they became like a kaleidoscopic collage of contrasts, yet a common thread bonded them together – their belief in the Jewish traditions, rites, rituals, their lifestyle and the dietary law.

I also discovered that almost all Jewish communities observe the Shabbath with handmade flatbread or chapatti or bread bought from a bakery, a bowl of salt and homemade grape sherbet for Shabbath prayers, followed by a sumptuous meal.

I noted that today, most Indian Jews rarely make traditional dishes for festivals or even the Shabbath. I hope that this book will inspire all generations of Indian Jews to return to their roots.

Coconut, and Coconut Milk, are an Important Part of
Indian Jewish Cuisine

A Note on the Recipes

According to the dietary law, chicken, mutton and fish are washed in salt water to remove all traces of blood. So, I will not detail this process in the recipes. In addition, I will not be mentioning that fish slices and chicken pieces are of medium size and mutton is cubed into 1 ½ inch-size pieces. Often, chicken is cut into pieces with legs, breast, wings and other preferred parts. Mutton is cubed from preferred parts like the thigh, flanks, shoulder, breast, ribs and is cooked on the bone. Sometimes, both chicken and mutton are cooked without bones, known as boneless. Except for 'malida' and 'chik cha halva,' the proportions used in the recipes are for four to five persons.

1

A Common Thread

Food is memory. Food is culture. Food bonds families and communities. It fades into childhood reminiscences and the nooks and corners of the past. Food is also part of our childhood. When a community decreases in number, its traditional food becomes a memory.

While studying the various aspects of Jewish food in India, I discovered some parallels. Most Jews came to India fleeing from persecution in Israel. They travelled by sea using different routes and settled in various regions, largely choosing coastal areas. Much before they settled in India, they had been living along the coast of present-day Israel. But when they were employed in various capacities during the British Raj, they settled in other landlocked parts of India. After the British left, they started building a new life in independent India. They chose different professions, as they were educated. Today, Indian Jews are employed in a variety of professions. Many are educationists, and there are very few Jews who are farmers like their ancestors. They prefer to stay closer to the areas where their forefathers had lived. So there are pockets where Indian Jews have settled, making sure that they have easy access to a synagogue.

The Bene Israel Jews settled by the Arabian Sea in Maharashtra and along rivers in Gujarat. The Cochin Jews chose the Kerala coastline. The Baghdadi Jews first settled in coastal Surat, then moved towards Mumbai and its seashore and then to Kolkata, along the Hooghly River in West Bengal. The Bene Ephraim Jews chose the seashores of Andhra Pradesh, while the Bnei Menashe Jews of Mizoram and Manipur chose to be by the lakes and mountains.

The food of the Indian Jews has regional influences but their staple diet is fish and rice. They observe the Jewish dietary law of not mixing meat with dairy products, so they mostly end their meals with fruit or sweet dishes like rice pudding with coconut milk or semolina halva. Separate utensils are allotted for milk and meat in their kitchens. They even avoid applying ghee on chapattis when meat dishes are made, to maintain the dietary law, as ghee is clarified butter, a dairy product. For festivals such as the Shabbath, grape-juice sherbet is made for the Kiddush or blessing. They also have a preference for succulent roe or fish eggs, often making them on special occasions or for guests. In the Jewish religion, fish is a symbol of protection, good luck, fertility and abundance.

Curries are often made with red or green masala, along with coconut milk as a substitute for dairy. The Jews of Mizoram and Manipur make soupy curries with meat, chicken and vegetables.

The Baghdadi Jews prefer to make desserts with agar-agar or China grass, which can be served with meat dishes.

Even if the Indian Jews live in geographically diverse areas and different landscapes, with varied food preferences – sometimes similar, sometimes not – they are bonded by their heritage of food.

Separate Vessels for Dairy-Based and Meat Dishes

2

A Secret Life: Being Indian and Jewish

It is impossible to write about Jewish food without mentioning the laws of kosher, which include slaughter of animals in a specific manner. The dietary laws also specify a list of clean and unclean birds and animals. It is prohibited to eat animals without cloven hooves. As mentioned before, there is a strict separation of meat and dairy in Jewish homes. Sometimes, kosher meat is not available in India, so many Indian Jews eat only vegetarian food through the year, waiting for special occasions or festivals when meat that has been slaughtered in accordance with the kosher law is available at the synagogue.

Some two thousand years ago, on their arrival in India, the Jews must have realized that coconut milk was the perfect substitute for dairy products. Rarely will you find a Bene Israel home that does not have coconut, lemon, tamarind and saffron in the kitchen, all of which which are commonly added to their curries.

Idol worship is prohibited in Judaism, but the Bene Israel Jews of western India have taken the liberty of worshipping Prophet Elijah, whose poster can be seen in their homes. They also have a ceremony for wish fulfilment, which is held for Prophet Elijah as a form of thanksgiving, known as malida. The entire community is invited to partake in a malida ceremony, for which a minyan of ten men is a must. Poha or flaked rice has a strong influence on Indian Jewish food and is an important ingredient of a malida platter. The poha is washed, mixed with grated coconut, garnished with raisins and chopped nuts, along with dates, apples, bananas or any other seasonal fruit, such as mangoes, and even with red rose petals. Sometimes an entire pomegranate is placed in the centre of the malida platter as a symbol of unity, or its seeds are sprinkled over the poha (Detailed recipe on pages 21–22).

The Bene Israel Jews also make a New Year halva known as chik-cha-halva. This is a wheat halva that is different from traditional Indian dairy-based sweets, though it does have a few similarities with Goan and Parsi desserts. This halva is a quintessential part of Bene Israel cuisine (Recipe on pages 47–49).

And, while matzo is available off the rack in Western countries, Indian Jews have always made their own hand-rolled flatbread, that is, matzo bread made with unleavened dough. Indian matzo is different from the matzo seen all over the world. Similarly, handrolled flatbread known as chapatti or bhakhri is made with wholewheat flour and has pride of place on the Shabbath table instead of the traditional challah bread made in Western countries. Interestingly, the traditional challah is available in the Kolkata-based Jewish bakery I visited.

In the absence of kosher wine in India, Jewish communities make sherbet with grapes or blackcurrants. The blackcurrants are washed, soaked in a bowl of water for ten minutes, drained, crushed, strained, cooled and then bottled (recipe on page 24). This juice is poured into a goblet for Kiddush during the Shabbath prayers; it is also made in large quantities for the Passover Seder and for breaking the fast of Yom Kippur.

The largest Indian Jewish community, the Bene Israel Jews, have been living in India for more than two thousand years. In Hebrew, Bene Israel means 'Children of Israel'. They came to India from Israel after the fall of King Solomon's second temple in 70 CE, fleeing from Greek persecution.

They were shipwrecked near Alibaug, where they continued to stay before they settled in Mumbai and western India. They kept their Biblical names but added the name of their village to their surnames. For example, my family comes from a village known as Danda, so my last name is Dandekar, which I do not use. They believe that India is their motherland, as it is the only country in the world where they have never faced persecution.

The Bene Israel Jews who settled on the Konkan coast worked as oilpressers in the villages around Alibaug, near Mumbai. They observed Shabbath from Friday evening to Saturday evening and were known as Shanivar telis or Saturday oilpressers.

As a memorial to the Bene Israel Jews, a tall column with a star-shaped pedestal was installed in Navgaon near Alibaug in 1992. It is built over two wells, which bear testimony to their arrival in India. It is known that even when they arrived in India, they would circumcise the male children and observe dietary laws. Slowly, the Bene Israel Jews assimilated into Indian life while absorbing some Indian customs, yet retaining their Jewish identity. The British and the Dutch recognized the Bene Israel Jews and gave them a religious education and books.

The Indian Jews have many Indian influences in their lifestyle, such as food habits, dress, jewellery and even cultural practices like the mehendi or henna ceremonies during weddings. Their rituals include the use of coconut, cloves, areca nut, areca leaves or paan leaves, myrtle leaves, the bijora or citron fruit, catnip leaves and local fragrant red roses. Maharashtrian, Konkani and Gujarati influences can also be seen in the apparel of the Bene Israel women, as they wear saris and bangles and weave flowers in their hair.

The Jewish communities in India stick to their roots in their celebrations of festivals and holidays. Jewish festivals are celebrated from September to August, such as the Jewish New Year or Rosh Hashanah, the Sukkot, Simchat Torah, Tisha-B'Av, Hanukkah, the Festival of Trees, Purim and Passover. Circumcisions, bar mitzvahs, engagements, weddings and naming ceremonies of newborn children feature a malida. The Shabbath spread is always made on a Friday evening, as the food must last till Saturday.

Bijora or Citron

3

The Bene Israel Jews of Western India

When I was writing my third novel, *Book of Esther*, I came to know that Alibaug in Raigad district, Maharashtra, was a major pilgrimage site for the Bene Israel Jews. I had been invited to a malida as a thanksgiving to Prophet Elijah – the prayers of which are known as Eliyahu Hannavi prayers – at Ahmedabad's Magen Abraham Synagogue. The cantor or hazzan, Joseph Samuel Pingle, fondly known as Johnybhai, had advised me to get in touch with Irene Abraham Samuel for information about how to reach Alibaug and where to stay over there. I met her and her husband, Abraham Joshua Samuel, at the synagogue in Ahmedabad. We spoke about Alibaug and the Rock of Prophet Elijah, and they gave me the phone numbers of her parents, Sophie and Samson David Wakrulkar, who live there. All I had to do was take a catamaran from the Gateway of India in Mumbai, reach Mandwa jetty in Alibaug and look out for Irene's parents.

From the Gateway of India, as I bought a ticket to board a boat, I could see Alibaug across the Mumbai harbour. As I walked towards the ferry, I saw the fishermen and boatmen sitting and chopping onions, green chillis and coriander leaves to make piping hot masala omelettes. The boat to Alibaug was like a chair car, from where I could see seagulls and the Alibaug coastline. The journey took about an hour.

This is how I reached Alibaug and discovered my Bene Israel homeland, where we had first arrived from Israel more than two thousand years ago.

Alibaug is a sleepy town by the sea, but most people dream about having a home there, overlooking the seashore. Its villages host several farmhouses belonging to the rich and famous who come from Mumbai on the weekends, where they indulge in cycling, jogging, horse-riding, relaxing and throwing parties for their celebrity friends.

The shimmering sea is an idyllic setting to tell the story of the arrival of Jews and how they settled down in India. Irene had told me that Alibaug has a synagogue and an ancient cemetery for its small Jewish community. Some synagogues in the villages around it are used for services, others are kept locked. Some Jewish families still have apartments, bungalows and cottage-like homes in the town.

Alibaug has a fish market, which always has a variety of fresh catch. On the outskirts of the villages, chikki is made by heating cauldrons of jaggery, which is mixed with peanuts or gram or grated coconut. There are provision stores, bakeries and much more, as the town keeps changing with the arrival of new residents.

I took a walk around Israel Street, where the Magen Aboth Synagogue stands, next to Sanman restaurant, which has one of the best seafood thalis in the area. Once, this street was well known for its masala factory and ice-cream soda stall. And, if one takes a luxury bus to Alibaug via the Pune Expressway, one can still have authentic ice-cream soda, the recipe of which is a closely guarded secret, at D'Samson's Cold Drinks, a stall run by a Bene Israel Jewish family.

Many villages in Maharashtra, such as Navgaon, Kehim, Awas and Jhirad, reflect the presence of the Bene Israel Jews, who adopted the village names as their surnames. Thus, you may hear the names Kehimkar, Awaskar or Navgaokar quite commonly within the community. The Bene Israel Jews have a strong Maharashtrian-Konkani influence on their lifestyles, dress and food habits. Most Bene Israel Jews speak Marathi amongst themselves, English and other regional languages in daily life, but all of them say their prayers in Hebrew. However, they say that Marathi is their mother tongue, and feel a deep connection to their Maharastrian roots.

When the Bene Israel Jews came to India, they had lost their holy books in the shipwreck, but they maintained an oral tradition, saying prayers like 'Shema Israel ... Hear O' Israel, the Lord our God, the Lord is One...', among others.

The story of Bene Israel Jews is connected with the arrival of David Rahabi in 1740. Dutch missionaries had heard about the presence of Bene Israel Jews in the Konkan area in 1738. A Cochin Jewish merchant, Ezekiel Rahabi, had written to the Jews of Amsterdam about the Bene Israel Jews of Konkan. His son David Rahabi, an agent of the Dutch East India Company, visited them in the mid eighteenth century and, it is believed, he discovered them, recognizing them as Jewish from some of their practices and he gave them religious education. He was asked by the British officials of the Raj to testify if the Bene Israel Jews belonged to the Jewish diaspora. In this way, the story of the Bene Israel Jews is connected with David Rahabi. Once the Bene Israelis were identified as Jews, they were employed in British and Dutch companies and given religious books, Torahs and prayer books in English, which were translated into Marathi. These books helped them follow Jewish customs, rites and rituals. Later, the Bene Israelis moved to Bombay, Pune and other cities, and were employed by the British East India Company. Their children went to missionary schools and colleges in 1813, where they learnt English and Hebrew.

Around 1857, a small community of Bene Israel Jews settled in Gujarat, especially Ahmedabad. Many of these families moved there while in service with the British. Others joined local textile mills and factories. Later, they became lawyers, doctors and educationists. Today, most Jews in Gujarat live in Ahmedabad, to be closer to the Magen Abraham Synagogue.

Surat, in Gujarat, also had several cemeteries of Bene Israel Jews and Baghdadi Jews, which have since been demolished.

Some Bene Israel Jews continue to live in Alibaug and practise their age-old profession of farming, as they own farms, fields and orchards.

Alibaug is known for the Navagaon cemetery, the site of the shipwreck, where some Jews are buried. The entry of the old cemetery at Navagaon was renovated in 2018 with donations received from Bene Israel Jews of India and Israel. An obelisk-like pillar, known as the Navagaon Memorial, marks the arrival of Bene Israel Jews in India and its entry is known as the Jerusalem Gate. Alibaug is also known for the Magen Aboth Synagogue and Beth El Synagogue in Revdanda.

The first synagogue in Mumbai, Sh'aar ha Rahamim or Gate of Mercy Synagogue, was built by Samuel Ezekiel Divekar in 1796. Later, many more synagogues were built in different parts of western India. They have distinct Indo-Jewish features or art deco styles of architecture. Some notable synagogues of Mumbai are the Tifereth Israel Synagogue, the Magen David Synagogue, the Knesset Eliyahu Synagogue, the Magen Hassidim Synagogue, the Rodef Shalom

Synagogue and the Shaar Hashamaim Synagogue or Gate of Heaven Synagogue. There are many synagogues in Mumbai and its suburbs, as Mumbai has the largest congregation of Bene Israel Jews in India. The Bene Israel Jews are largely cosmopolitan, as they live in different areas around Mumbai. Many members of the community live in suburban Thane, close to the Shaar Hashamim Synagogue, where they have regular services.

Pen and Panvel near Mumbai also have some synagogues from where some Jewish organizations are involved in the management of an old people's home, as well as in hosting activities for Jewish youth groups. These organizations take these groups on tours to Israel and other European countries, to educate them about Jewish history. They also host Jewish visitors from abroad, taking them to Jewish sites and introducing them to Indian life. Often, interactive workshops are held on various aspects of Judaism as well. Generally speaking, Mumbai is the centre of most activities connected with Bene Israel Jewish life in India. This is also due to the fact that the Israeli consulate is situated in Mumbai. The consulate helps indigenous Jews to meet Jewish dignitaries and rabbis from abroad. Through the consulate, they are exposed to various aspects of Judaism, the celebration of festivals and community activities. Jewish tourists regularly come to India to visit Jewish destinations. Besides cities like Mumbai, Kochi and Kolkata, Alibaug has also become part of their itinerary.

In India, the hazzan or cantor of the synagogue and the shamash or messengers were provided housing near the synagogue, according to an old Jewish practice. Earlier, when a synagogue had a shamash, he was also given housing and a scooter to visit Jewish homes and give them information about events at the synagogue. In Ahmedabad, the last shamash of the Magen Abraham Synagogue, Daniel Reuben, passed away in 2011. And, in recent times, the custom of employing a shamash at a synagogue is no longer prevalent; instead, Jewish events are circulated over social media. Some of the Bene Israel Jewish women of Mumbai, Ahmedabad and Alibaug have taken to catering for the malida ceremony, apart from other festivals and community dinners.

Judaism is based on the Torah, but an unusual feature of the Bene Israel Jews is an intense belief in Prophet Elijah, also known as Eliyahu Hannabi. It is a bonding factor for them. Prophet Elijah is a Biblical hero whose miraculous ascent to heaven is connected with the much-awaited arrival of the messiah. He is a beloved folk hero of the Bene Israel Jews of India. Rarely will you find a Bene Israel home that does not have a picture of Prophet Elijah. Typically, the picture shows the long-haired, white-bearded prophet dressed in a rose-pink robe with a blue mantle, riding in a chariot of fire driven by two powerful white stallions rising towards heaven in a cloud, surrounded by cherubs and angels. Down below on earth, one can see the silhouette of Jerusalem – or could it be Alibaug, where the Bene Israel Jews first landed after the shipwreck? Throughout Jewish history, Prophet Elijah has been associated with relieving the suffering of Jews and bringing closer the day of redemption. The Bene Israel Jews believe that Prophet Elijah ascended to heaven from a site near present-day Haifa in Israel, and that while he was on his way to heaven, he flew over India, stopping at Khandala, which is near Alibaug. It is believed that the Prophet departed on his chariot from a rock-shaped platform, leaving on it the imprint of his horses' hooves and chariot wheels. This rock edict is revered by the Bene Israel Jews as a pilgrimage site known as Eliyahu Hannabi cha Tapa or Rock of Elijah, where they make vows for wish fulfilment, followed by a malida.

While living in India, a land of so many gods, the Bene Israel elders may have decided to start worshipping Prophet Elijah to keep the Jewish community together. The prophet is invoked by Bene Israel Jews at every auspicious occasion and most synagogues have an ornate chair on display, specially kept aside for the prophet.

Food and language normally tell us who we are and from where we come, as both open doors to traditions, rituals, beliefs and life. Often, food is like an introduction and sets the tone for a conversation. Like most Jews of India and abroad, the Bene Israel Jews follow the dietary law.

The use of coconut milk as a substitute for dairy worked perfectly in their cuisine. This also marked the beginning of the influence of Maharashtrian or Konkani food on Jewish cuisine. Sometimes, coconut milk is made at home with grated coconut, which is soaked in warm water and strained, or processed in a mixer with water before being strained. And, when in a hurry, tinned coconut milk is bought from a supermarket.

When kosher meat is not easily available, Bene Israel Jews have vegetarian food. On special occasions or festivals, meat is available at synagogues, prepared in accordance with the dietary law. In the absence of a shohet, elders of the community prepare meat in a specific manner, according to the dietary law. Often, the hazzan prepares kosher meat for the community. Among meat dishes, the Bene Israel Jews have a preference for chicken, mutton and fish.

Like many Indians, the Bene Israel Jews prefer a meal of dal, rice, chapattis and vegetables, with or without fish or chicken. When it comes to types of fish, they have a special preference for pomfret and bombil or Bombay duck.

Most Indian Jews are addicted to tea, popularly known as chai. To make chai, water is boiled in a vessel, sugar is added with tea leaves, brewed for a few minutes, milk is added and boiled till the tea has a rich brown colour, poured into cups and served with savoury snacks or fritters like hot pakodas, which are popularly made with potatoes, onions or other vegetables. Tea is also made with mint leaves and grated ginger, with or without cardamom seeds.

Some families serve service tea in a tray, with brewed black tea in a teapot, along with a milk jug, sugar bowl, teacups and teaspoons. The host serves tea according to the preference of each guest.

Bene Israel Jewish families keep aside the vessels used to make tea, so that the flavour of the tea remains pure. In this process they follow the dietary law, as milk is added to the tea and meat dishes are never cooked in vessels used to make tea.

FESTIVALS AND OCCASIONS

Shabbath

The Shabbath is the focal point of Jewish life and bonds them with their family and community. The Shabbath table is covered with a clean tablecloth and decorated with two candles. Bread, a goblet of wine for Kiddush and platters of food are always part of the spread. It is an occasion for joy, light and peace. It is a Jewish tradition which signifies hope for a better future. Some Jews observe Shabbath from Friday evening to Saturday evening. Shabbath is a day of rest, as it is the seventh day of the Jewish week, beginning at sundown on Friday and lasting up to sundown on Saturday. It is a day when Jews are not to work, because according to the Jewish Bible,

...And God saw everything that he had made; and behold, it was very good. And the evening and the morning were the sixth day ... Thus the heavens and the earth ... were finished, and everything in them was completed ... And on the seventh day God ended his work which he had made; and he rested on the seventh day from all his work which he had made.[1]

All around the world, on Friday night, most Jewish families and Jewish congregations observe Shabbath with a service, either at home or at the synagogue.

Indian Jews make sherbet with blackcurrants for Kiddush prayers whereas in most Western countries, wine is used for the prayers. Challah or plaited bread is made for the Shabbath prayers as well. In recent years, in India, many Jewish women have learnt to bake challah at home. Order-based challah bread is available in Mumbai through some Jewish organizations.

On Friday evening, the woman of the house lights two candles for Shabbath, peace and togetherness, while prayers are said over bread (this can be flatbread or bhakhri or store-bought bread), as the Kiddush is said over a goblet of blackcurrant sherbet. The sherbet is then had by the family, followed by a sumptous meal.

Woman of the House Lighting the Shabbath Candles

1   The Book of Genesis 1

Purim

This festival is celebrated to mark the liberation of Persian Jews from Haman by the queen of Persia, Queen Esther. Purim falls on a full moon night and is celebrated in India, often on the same night as Holi, the Indian festival of colours. It is celebrated with puran polis or sweet flatbread, which is often made at home or at the synagogue by a Jewish caterer.

Rosh Hashanah

The Jewish New Year is the anniversary of the earth's creation. On this day, it is customary to have pieces of apples dipped in honey to sweeten the year ahead. The Bene Israel Jews also make an unusual sweet, chik-cha-halva, to celebrate the new year. This rather rubbery sweet is made with coconut milk, wheat extract and sugar. Dry wheat extract is made or bought from speciality shops. The mixture is boiled for hours, then spread in thalis, cooled, cut into diamond shapes and decorated with nuts and rose petals. This delicious pink halva captures the essence of Bene Israel cuisine. The next day, a shofar or ram's horn is blown in synagogues all over the world to welcome the new year, leading towards the Day of Atonement or Yom Kippur.

Yom Kippur

These are days of penitence, repentance and self-examination. It is customary to fast from sundown on the eve of Yom Kippur till the next evening. According to ancient Jewish texts, during the Day of Atonement, prayers are said to seek forgiveness from God for wrongs done during the year.

The Bene Israel Jews make kippur-chi-puri to break the fast of Yom Kippur. These crescent-shaped puris are similar to the

Maharashtrian karanjis or sweet puris, which are made with a filling of grated coconut or semolina, sugar and nuts, and then fried in ghee or vegetable oil (detailed recipe on pages 50–52).

Kippur Chi Puri

Sukkot

This is known as the Feast of Tabernacles. It commemorates the forty-year-long journey of the Jews through the desert to Israel. To celebrate this, back in the day, Jews took offerings from their first harvest as a gift to the temple, in gratitude to God for blessing the land with abundance and prosperity. Sukkot is observed by dwelling in a tent, which is constructed in the courtyard of a synagogue. The ceiling of the tent is made with palm fronds and decorated with a variety of fruits tied inside the ceiling of the tent with the holy citrus, etrog, known as bijora in western India. A 'loot' is held on the last day of Sukkot, where the young man who grabs the citrus is said to be bestowed with a blessing which will fulfil his secret wishes.

Shavout

This festival is celebrated to rejoice the receiving of the Ten Commandments on Mount Sinai. In India, it is observed by making carrot halva or bottle-gourd halva or modak.

The Festival of Trees

This festival is also known as the New Year of Trees. It is celebrated during the harvest season with a malida platter, which is filled with fragrant red roses, dates, bananas, apples and sweetened poha and garnished with grated coconut and chopped nuts (recipe on pages 21–22). To make it festive, seasonal fruits like berries, grapes and strawberries are arranged on the platter and served to the congregation, followed by a vegetarian meal.

Passover

Passover is a spring festival and celebrates the exodus of Jews from Egypt. It is observed for seven days by eating unleavened bread or matzo to remind Jews of the flight from Egypt and freedom from slavery. During Passover, the Book of Exodus is read out by the cantor of the synagogue or an elder at home, in memory of the time when Jews were slaves in Egypt. It recounts how Moses led them to freedom. It is a constant source of inspiration for Jews all over the world. If celebrated at home, a traditional Passover table or Seder is set with a ritualistic meal. The Seder table is decorated with flowers, candles, a fresh tablecloth; the special Passover platter covered with an embroidered cloth. The dining table is set with the best, shining, sparkling and festive tableware. When Passover is held at a synagogue, the main table is set for the hazzan or cantor and the other tables are arranged for the congregation. Indian matzo or unleavened bread, known as bin-khameer-chi-bhakhri, is kept in a matzo cover on the Seder platter (recipe on page 25–26). This unleavened bread is made in Bene Israel households as a symbol of the time when Jews were slaves in Egypt. They carried this bread with their meagre belongings when they crossed the Red Sea. It is different from matzo bread, which is easily available in Israel and other Western countries. Nowadays, some Jewish organizations in Mumbai receive matzo from Israel and send boxes of it to other synagogues in India.

Simchat Torah

This festival marks the completion of the annual cycle of Torah readings. As, part of the festivities, the Bene Israel Jews organize a fancy dress competition and participants dress like Biblical characters. Sometimes they follow Indian themes. It is also celebrated with dancing and singing.

Non-vegetarian meals are made for Simchat Torah.

Tisha B'Av

This festival is observed with a fast and is held in memory of the destruction of King Solomon's first and second temples in Jerusalem. A dish known as birda is made with sprouted val beans or flat beans and is served with puris to break the fast of Tisha B'Av (recipe on page 38–39).

Hanukkah

This Jewish festival of lights is celebrated in memory of Jewish victory over Greek invasion. A special nine-pronged lamp or menorah is kindled every night during the eight days of Hannukah to commemorate the re-dedication of the temple in Jerusalem, either at home or at the synagogue. Savoury snacks like samosas or pakoras or fritters are served along with carrot halva during this festival. Often, the Bene Israel Jews enact a costume drama based on the Biblical theme of Hanukkah.

Malida

Malida is prepared as a thanksgiving to Prophet Elijah by the Bene Israel Jews of western India, for wish fulfilment.

Ten Jewish men, known as a minyan, have to be present for a malida. Often, the entire community is invited for a malida, which is followed by dinner. A malida is often held at a synagogue or a Jewish home between 7 to 8 p.m. Hence, preparations start in the pavilion of the synagogue by midday. Chairs are arranged for the congregation along with long tables, so that women can prepare the malida, which can be held at home or at a rented hall, like the one at The Rock of Prophet Elijah or Eliyahoo Hannabi cha Tapa in Sagav village, Alibaug. Groups of Bene Israel Jews from India and Israel often hold a malida at this pilgrimage site.

RECIPES

Malida Platter

Ingredients

> Basmati poha or flattened rice – 500 grams
> Powdered sugar – 400 grams
> Coconut – 1
> Raisins – 20 grams
> Cashew nuts – 20 grams
> Pistachio – 20 grams
> Almonds – 20 grams
> Chironji seeds – 20 grams
> Cardamom powder – 1 tablespoon
> Nutmeg powder – ¼ teaspoon
> Red roses – 30
> Dates – 30
> Bananas – 15

Apples – 5

Green grapes – 500 grams

Oranges – 5

Chikoos – 8

Guavas – 8

Method

Place the poha in a colander and wash under running water; drain and remove excess water. Transfer poha into a deep vessel. Mix with powdered sugar, freshly grated coconut, finely chopped nuts, cardamom powder and nutmeg powder. Cover the vessel with a lid and keep aside. Keep the fruit in separate vessels, with bananas cut into halves, sliced apples, sliced mangoes, sliced chikoos, sliced guavas, segmented oranges, individual grapes and seedless dates. In a big platter, place the apples in the centre with desi red roses and make a circular arrangement with the bananas, seedless dates, grapes, oranges, chikoo, guava, mangoes or any other seasonal fruit. Sometimes a pomegranate is placed in the centre as a symbol of unity. Arrange the poha around the fruit.

When prayers end at the synagogue and the congregation returns to the pavilion, women fill quarter-plates with the roses, fruit and poha. The hazzan chants blessings over a rose, known as 'phool chi baraka', followed by the 'Ha'etz' or fruit which grows on trees with hard trunks, like dates, and the 'Ha'adama' or fruit which grows on trees with soft trunks, like bananas. These are served with other fruits, followed by a prayer for sweetened poha or 'malida chi baraka,' as volunteers offer malida plates to the congregation. After this a sumptuous dinner is served.

Optional: Seasonal fruits such as melons, strawberries and berries.

Shabbath

Hamotzi or Shabbath Bhakhri

Ingredients

   Wheat flour – 1 cup
   Oil – 1 tablespoon
   Water – ½ cup
   Salt to taste

Method

Place one cup of flour in a wide-rimmed steel platter. Add oil, water, knead into a firm dough, cover and keep aside for ten minutes. Divide the dough into small balls, place each ball on a board and, with a rolling pin, roll out into a flatbread about four inches in circumference. Place the flatbread on an iron griddle, roast on both sides until bhakhri is slightly crisp, remove from stove and store in a chapatti box.

For Shabbath prayers, one bhakhri is kept on a plate and covered with a ceremonial cloth, which is uncovered when the prayers begin. The bhakhri is sprinkled with salt for the prayers, then broken into smaller pieces and offered to family and friends present for Shabbath. Since ancient times, salt is had with bread, as it was added to all offerings made at the Temple in Israel.

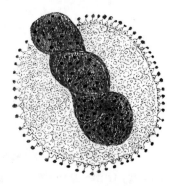

Shabbath Bhakhri

Shabbath Sherbet

In India, most Jewish families make homemade sherbet for Shabbath prayers and Jewish festivals.

Ingredients

    Black seedless dry grapes – 500 grams
    Water – 1 litre

Method

Wash dried black seedless grapes in a colander till clean. Soak them in a bowl of water from early morning to late afternoon (seven to nine hours). Then process in a mixer, strain through a thin muslin cloth or fine-mesh strainer, bottle and keep in a refrigerator.

At sunset, the sherbet is poured into a goblet for the Kiddush prayers. The person who says the Kiddush sips sherbet from the goblet and passes it to family and friends present for Shabbath prayers. Sometimes, smaller shot glasses are filled with sherbet for guests. The sherbet stays fresh in the fridge for two days.

Indian Jews make this sherbet as kosher wine is not available.

Optional: Sugar as per taste.

Kanavali or Shabbath Cake

Ingredients

    Semolina – 500 grams
    Ghee or vegetable oil – ½ cup
    Coconut milk – 1 litre
    Water – 1 litre
    Jaggery – 250 grams
    Cardamom powder – 1 teaspoon
    Raisins and chopped dry fruit – 2 tablespoons

Method

This cake is made with semolina. Heat ghee in a heavy-bottomed kadhai and add semolina. Roast the mixture on a slow fire till golden brown. Add sugar or chopped jaggery and a pinch of salt. Pour coconut milk over this mixture and stir continuously till the liquid evaporates and the semolina absorbs the ghee. Garnish with cardamom powder, raisins, finely chopped almonds and cashew nuts. Cover the kadhai with a lid and cook the semolina for a few more minutes, then transfer onto a greased flat baking tray, place in an oven and bake at 180 degrees Celsius for ten minutes.

Remove from the oven, cool, cut into diamond-shaped pieces and serve.

In the absence of an oven, pour the semolina mixture into a thali or platter, cover with a lid, then place in a heavy-bottomed pan, which is half-filled with water. Cook for about fifteen minutes on a medium flame, then cool, cut into diamond-shaped pieces and serve.

If the kanavali is made on Friday afternoon, the leftovers are served the next day for Shabbath lunch. As the cake is made with ghee, it is served only with vegetarian dishes. Nowadays, due to time constraints, this cake and many other recipes mentioned here are rarely made in Jewish homes.

Passover Recipes

Bin-Khameer-Chi-Bhakri

Ingredients

> Wheat flour – 1 cup
> Water – ½ cup

Method

Sift the wheat flour without salt or yeast and make into a stiff dough by mixing with water. Divide into balls and roll on a board with a rolling-pin into medium-size chapattis and keep aside. Roast these on a heavy iron griddle or clay pan or tava, which is placed upside down on a stove, till chapattis are crisp on both sides.

The first chapatti is rolled from the dough according to the recipe given above. Then, with the pressure of a thumb, a fingertip-sized cap is made on one side of the chapatti. Roast it on the griddle or tava and keep aside. This cap represents the priests or Cohens who were allowed to enter the inner sanctuary of the Temple in ancient times.

The second chapatti is given two fingertip-sized M-shaped caps, to represent the Levis or soldiers.

The third chapatti is given three-rounded-fingertip-size-caps, to represent the Israelis.

Indian Date Sheera or Haroset

Ingredients

Seedless dates – 5 cups
Water – 5 cups

Method

Pressure-cook the dates with water for 5 to 6 whistles, strain, transfer onto a pan and cook on a low flame till they soften. Mash them with a hand masher into pulp and simmer for five minutes until dry. Put in a bowl and place in the Passover platter. It is symbolic of the mortar used by Jews to build the pyramids for the Pharaohs when they were slaves.

Leftovers are bottled and kept in the fridge for two to three days and served with bread or chapattis.

Seder Platter

Jerova

After a goat is slaughtered, the thighbone is removed and the meat attached to the bone is cleaned. The bone is washed, roasted on an open flame and placed in the Seder platter. The bone is symbolic of the sacrificial lamb and is offered to the Lord as thanksgiving, commemorating the time when the Jews came to dwell in their ancestral land after many years of wandering in the desert. It is a holy offering and not edible.

A roasted leg of chicken can also be placed in the platter as an alternative to the goat thighbone.

Karpas and Maror

Clean, wash and dry parsley and salad leaves, and place in the platter with a bowl of lemon juice. Bitter herbs are placed in the Seder platter as a reminder of the misery and hardship Jews suffered when they were slaves in Egypt.

Limbu-cha-ras

Wash, halve and juice fresh lemons. Mix the juice with water and serve in small bowls, according to an ancient tradition, so that each person can dip boiled eggs, parsley or lettuce in the lemon juice and eat them. This ritual of placing lemon juice in the Passover platter symbolizes the tears shed by the Jews when they were slaves in Egypt. It also represents spring and the renewal of life.

Variation: Sometimes bowls of salt water are placed in the Passover platter instead of lemon juice.

Boiled Egg

A boiled egg with its shell intact is roasted on an open fire and placed in the Seder platter, as eggs are symbolic of the cycle of life. According to the number of people present, some more eggs are boiled, peeled and kept in the Passover platters on each table for the number of people attending the Seder.

Chicken and Meat Recipes

Chicken Curry

Ingredients

Chicken – 500 grams

Oil – ½ cup

Onions – 2

Bay leaf – 1

Tomatoes – 2

Ginger-garlic paste – 1 tablespoon

Grated coconut – 1 heaped tablespoon

Cashew and dried melon-seed paste – 2 tablespoons

Red chilli powder – 2 teaspoons

Turmeric – 1 teaspoon

Cumin-coriander powder – 1 tablespoon

Garam masala – 1 tablespoon

Lemon – 1

Coriander leaves

Water – 1 ½ glass

Salt to taste

Method

Wash chicken pieces and keep aside. In a bowl, mix finely chopped onions, cubed tomatoes, grated coconut, the cashew nut and dried melon-seed paste, red chilli powder, turmeric, cumin-coriander powder and garam masala. Blend in a processer with 1 tablespoon water to make a thick paste. Heat oil in a casserole; temper with bay leaf, ginger-garlic paste, processed masala and salt, and cook on a low flame for seven to eight minutes. Add the chicken pieces and water, stir, cover, cook on a medium flame for ten minutes. Reduce flame, simmer for twenty minutes on a low flame till the sauce thickens and chicken is tender. Add the lemon juice and garnish with coriander leaves. Serve hot with rice.

Mutton Curry

Ingredients

Mutton – 500 grams

Oil – ½ cup

Onions – 2

Tomatoes – 2

Ginger-garlic paste – 2 tablespoons

Grated coconut – 1 heaped tablespoon

Dried melon-seed and cashew nut paste – 2 tablespoons

Red chilli powder – 1 tablespoon

Turmeric powder – 1 teaspoon

Cumin-coriander powder – 1 tablespoon

Garam masala – 1 tablespoon

Water – 1½ glasses

Lemon – 1

Coriander leaves for garnish

Salt to taste

Method

Wash cubed mutton pieces and keep aside. Heat 1 tablespoon oil in a casserole, add the sliced onions and fry till brown. Transfer with a slotted spoon into a bowl, mix with finely chopped tomatoes, freshly grated coconut, the melon seed and cashew nut paste and process in a mixer with 1 tablespoon water to make a paste. Put the mixture back into the same bowl.

Heat 2 tablespoons oil in the same casserole. Add the processed mixture, sauté, add red chilli powder, turmeric, cumin-coriander powder, garam masala and salt to taste. Add mutton, stir, cover with lid and cook on a low flame for thirty minutes. Add the lemon juice, stir, cook on a medium flame for ten minutes till the gravy thickens and mutton is tender. Garnish with coriander leaves and serve hot with wheat- or rice-flour chapattis and rice.

Mince Cutlet

Ingredients

Minced mutton – 300 grams

Boiled potatoes – 7 medium

Onions – 1 medium

Ginger-garlic, finely diced – 1 tablespoon

Cumin – 1 teaspoon

Red chilli powder – 1 teaspoon

Oil – ½ cup for shallow frying

Green chillis, finely chopped – 1 teaspoon

Coriander leaves, finely chopped – 2 tablespoons

Eggs – 2

Breadcrumbs – 2 cups

Method

Wash the minced meat, pressure-cook for forty minutes and keep aside. Heat some of the oil in a pan and fry the finely chopped onions, along with ginger-garlic paste, cumin, red chilli powder, finely diced green chillis and chopped coriander leaves. Add this to the precooked minced meat and cook till dry. Remove from the stove and cool. Alongside, boil the potatoes, mash and mix with salt. Divide this mixture into lemon-sized balls and shape into cup-size puries. Put the minced filling inside each puri, close the puri over the meat, then shape into round medium-sized cutlets and keep aside.

In another bowl, beat the eggs, then dip the cutlets in the egg wash, coat with breadcrumbs and keep aside. The cutlets are now ready to fry. Heat oil in a pan and shallow-fry the cutlets till they are golden brown. These cutlets are often served as a starter or as a snack with drinks.

Variation: The Bene Israel Jews also make vegetable pattice, cutlets, pakodas and samosas during community dinners. Vegetable cutlets can be similarly made with mashed potatoes, peas and carrots.

Fish Recipes

Fried Fish Heads

Ingredients

Oil – 2 tablespoons
Fish heads – 4
Red chilli powder – 1 teaspoon
Salt to taste
Water

Method

Fish heads are made for the Jewish New Year or Rosh Hashanah. This recipe is used for the fish head, while the rest of the fish is used to make fried fish or fish curry.

Wash the fish heads, place in a plate and marinate with salt, lemon juice and red chilli powder. Heat oil in a pan and shallow-fry the fish heads for three minutes. Flip and simmer on a low flame for three more minutes till tender and remove from the stove.

This is served as an accompaniment to the New Year meal, which comprises chicken curry or mutton curry served with rice.

Fish in Red Masala Curry

Ingredients

Fish pieces – 500 grams
Oil – 2 tablespoons
Onion – 1
Garlic – 2 cloves
Turmeric – 1 teaspoon

Red chilli powder – 1½ teaspoons

Tomato puree – ¼ cup

Coconut milk – 1 cup

Curry leaves – 4

Fresh coriander leaves – 1 tablespoon

Method

Wash fish slices and soak in water for ten minutes. Keep aside.

In a blender, process the finely chopped onion, diced garlic cloves, tomato puree, red chilli powder and salt, and make a paste. Heat oil in a casserole and add this masala paste. Cook on a low flame, add fish slices and then cook on a medium flame for five minutes till the fish is tender. Add coconut milk, simmer on a low flame for three minutes till the gravy has a bright red runny consistency. Add curry leaves, garnish with coriander leaves, remove casserole from stove and serve with rice.

Optional: The same recipe can be made with chicken with a longer cooking time for the chicken to tenderize.

Fish in Green Masala Curry

Ingredients

Fish pieces – 500 grams

Turmeric – 1 teaspoon

Coriander-cumin powder – 1 tablespoon

Grated coconut – 1 tablespoon

Potato – 1

Tomatoes – 2

Green chillies – 3

Ginger-garlic paste – 1 tablespoon

Curry leaves – 3–4

Coriander leaves – 150 grams

Mint leaves – 3–4

Lemon juice – 1 ½ tablespoons

Cocum petals – 4

Salt to taste

Method

Wash fish slices and keep aside.

In a mixer, process chopped tomato, grated coconut, green chillies, ginger-garlic paste, coriander-cumin powder, mint leaves, fresh coriander leaves and keep aside.

Heat oil in a heavy-bottomed casserole, temper with curry leaves, add the processed masala and sauté on a low flame. Add 1 peeled and cubed potato. When the potato is almost cooked, add the fish pieces and simmer on a low flame. Add the lemon juice, cocum petals and 1 glass of water and cook on a medium flame for seven to eight minutes. Remove from stove and serve with rice.

Optional: Tamarind juice can be added instead of cocum petals. When the fish is half-cooked, add a pinch of black pepper powder and simmer for a few minutes.

Variation: The same recipe can be made with chicken or poached eggs.

Fish Alberas

Alberas is now rarely made in Bene Israel homes. In earlier times, when the Bene Israel Jewish women of western India would decide to make Alberas, it was understood that it needed a lot of preparation and ingredients. With time, Alberas became a forgotten recipe. While researching about it, I found that some Jewish women of Alibaug, Mumbai and Ahmedabad had fond memories about their grandmothers making this dish for the family. This is how the recipe of Alberas came to me. Alberas means making fish with the maximum amount of ingredients. In earlier times, the masala was not processed in a mixer, but the ingredients were finely diced or roughly ground in a stone mortar with a pestle.

Ingredients

    Fish pieces – 500 grams
    Onion – 1
    Oil – ¼ cup
    Garlic cloves – 5
    Ginger – 1 inch
    Coconut milk – 1 cup
    Red chilli powder – 1 teaspoon
    Turmeric powder – 1 teaspoon
    Cumin-coriander powder – 1 teaspoon
    Green chilli – 1
    Tomatoes – 2
    Potato – 1
    Cocum – 4 petals
    Lemon – 1
    Coriander leaves – 1 tablespoon
    Mint – 2–3 leaves
    Salt to taste

Method

Wash the fish slices in water. Peel potatoes and cut them and the tomatoes into roundels and sprinkle with salt. Heat oil in a deep vessel on a low flame and brown the onions, along with finely chopped ginger-garlic and green chillies. Layer this mixture with the potatoes, ½ cup of coconut milk and 1 cup water, and cook till the potatoes soften. Place the fish slices and tomatoes over the potatoes, cook with the remaining coconut milk on a low flame for seven minutes till the fish is tender and the sauce thickens. Garnish with finely chopped coriander leaves and mint leaves. Remove from stove and serve with coconut rice.

Fried Fish

Ingredients

> Fish – 500 grams
> Oil – ½ cup
> Red chilli powder – 1 teaspoon
> Turmeric powder – 1 teaspoon
> Cumin-coriander powder – 1 teaspoon
> Lemon – 1
> Ginger-garlic paste – 1 ½ teaspoon
> Rice flour – 25 grams
> Salt to taste

Method

Clean the fish pieces, soak in water, drain and place on a platter. Extract the juice of 1 lemon, mix with salt and rub over fish slices. Marinate the fish for 1 hour. Then place it in a colander, so that the excess juices are drained. Cover the fish slices with rice flour mixed with cumin-coriander powder, ginger-garlic paste and salt. Heat oil in a kadhai, fry the fish till tender and crisp, remove with slotted spoon and serve with chapattis or dal and rice.

Fish-egg Roe Cutlets

Ingredients

Fish eggs – 500 grams
Oil – 2 tablespoons
Black pepper powder – 1 teaspoon
Egg – 1
Breadcrumbs – 100 grams
Salt to taste

Method

Wash the fish eggs carefully, and sprinkle with turmeric and salt. Steam-cook till done, cool, remove from cooker, place on a plate and cut into medium-sized pieces.

In a separate bowl, crack and beat the eggs. Dip each fish-egg piece in the egg wash; cover with breadcrumbs and keep aside on a plate. Heat oil is heated in a pan and fry.

Optional: Red chilli powder can also be sprinkled on the fish eggs before they are steamed.

Bombay Duck or Bombil

The Bene Israel Jews have a special preference for Bombay duck, which is also known as bombil. The bombil is a small eel-like fish that is soft and fleshy. A pinkish-red colour on its head indicates its freshness, and this is what one looks out for when purchasing it from the market. Bombil are sometimes sun-dried, salted and stored in an airy container, so that they are always handy to make a quick dinner. They can be served as an accompaniment to khichdi on a Saturday night, when Shabbath ends. When dried, they have a strong fishy smell.

The bombil can also be shallow fried. It has one bone, which is removed carefully, while its fine white scales have to be scraped. Sometimes, its head is removed during preparation. The fish is then halved and salted. The excess moisture from the fish is removed by keeping it under a weight, preferably a stone mortar, which also flattens the flesh of the bombil. The halves of the fish are then washed, patted dry and rubbed with lemon juice and salt, before being coated with a rice-flour mixture that has been seasoned with turmeric and chilli powder. Oil is heated in a pan and the bombils is shallow-fried till golden brown and crisp.

Egg and Vegetarian Recipes

Fried Egg

I saw another version of the normal fried egg while staying in a Bene Israel Jewish home in Alibaug. It was made in small steel bowls known as vatki or katori. Oil was heated in the steel bowl, on a low flame, and a little ghee was added to the hot oil. An egg was broken and dropped into this bowl, which was held over the flame with a steel holder till the egg was done, sunny side up. Then, with a small steel spatula, the egg was removed onto a plate and served with chapattis or bread.

Flat Beans or Birda

Ingredients

　　Val beans or bitter field beans – 1 cup
　　Oil – 2 tablespoons
　　Onion – 1
　　Tomato – 1 large

Green chilli – 1

Garlic – ½ teaspoon

Ginger – ½ teaspoon

Red chilli powder – ½ teaspoon

Turmeric –¼ teaspoon

Cumin powder – ½ teaspoon

Coriander powder – ½ teaspoon

Coconut milk – ½ cup

Garam masala – 1 teaspoon

Fresh coriander leaves – 2 tablespoons

Water – 1 cup

Salt to taste

Method

In a vessel of warm water, soak 1 cup of bitter val beans for ten hours. When the beans soften, drain the water, and tie them in a damp muslin cloth bag. Hang on a hook and periodically sprinkle water, as the beans take two days to sprout.

When the val beans sprout, remove from the cloth bag, wash, drain, peel, wash again and pressure-cook in 2 cups of water for twenty-five minutes till soft and keep aside.

In a kadhai, heat the oil, add 1 finely chopped onion and sauté till transparent. Add the ginger-garlic paste, diced green chillis, chopped tomato and simmer on a low flame till soft. Add red chilli powder, cumin, turmeric, garam masala, salt and stir. Add the val beans, 1 cup water, 1 cup coconut milk, mix and cook on a medium flame for ten minutes till the gravy thickens. Garnish with fresh coriander leaves and serve with sweet puris (recipe on pages 50–52).

Note: Val beans are made to break the fast of Tisha B'Av.

Tilkut Potatoes

This recipe is a family favourite, which was handed to me by my grandmother Shebabeth. Tilkut masala is made with a mixture of powdered sesame and red chilli powder. Home-made tilkut stays for six months in a bottle. Some Bene Israel Jewish families make tilkut chutney with red chillies, sesame seeds, garlic, raw peanuts and salt, which are mixed with oil and served as an accompaniment to some dishes.

Ingredients

Potatoes – 7

Tilkut powder – 1 ¾ tablespoons

Onions – 2

Spring onions – 4

Oil – 1 cup

Whole sesame seeds for garnishing – 1 tablespoon

Salt to taste

Method

Peel the potatoes and slice. Heat oil in a heavy kadhai, in which sesame seeds are tempered. Add the potatoes and cook on a high flame. Stir continuously till the potatoes are half done, after which lower the flame and cover the kadhai. Cook the potatoes for another five to ten minutes. Then add sliced onions with tilkut powder, salt and chopped spring onions. Cover the kadhai once again and cook till done. Drain any excess oil and cook the potatoes for five more minutes till crisp. This dish is served hot with khichdi or chapattis or bread or with a plain dal-and-rice combination or with yogurt or yogurt-based kadhi and khichdi.

Optional: Tilkut potatoes can be made without spring onions but, if available, they give a fresh flavour to this recipe.

Note: For 7 potatoes, you need tilkut powder made with 1 tablespoon chilli powder and 3/4 teaspoon sesame seeds. And 1 tablespoon whole sesame seeds is used for garnishing.

Chauli Beans or Black-eyed Beans Curry

Ingredients

- Chauli beans – 1 cup
- Oil – 2 tablespoons
- Onion – 1
- Ginger-garlic paste – 1 ½ teaspoons
- Tomato – 1
- Turmeric – ½ teaspoon
- Red chilli powder – 1 teaspoon
- Cumin-coriander powder – 2 teaspoons
- Garam masala – 1 teaspoon
- Coconut milk – ½ cup
- Coriander leaves – 1 tablespoon
- Water – 3 ½ glasses
- Salt to taste

Method

In a vessel of water, soak chauli beans overnight.

Next day, drain and wash the beans and keep aside. In the same vessel where the beans were kept, add 1 glass of water, add the beans again, boil, cover with a lid and cook for twenty-five minutes till soft.

In another vessel, heat the oil, add finely chopped onions and cook till transparent. Add ginger-garlic paste, stir, simmer on a low flame. Add finely chopped tomatoes and cook till soft. Add powdered turmeric, red chilli powder, cumin-coriander powder and garam masala and mix. Add the beans, stir and cook on a low flame for five minutes. Add 1 cup water and the coconut milk, mix well and cook on a medium flame till the gravy thickens. Garnish with finely chopped fresh coriander leaves and serve hot with rice.

Note: Bene Israel Jews make chauli beans during festivals and weddings.

Fried Eggplant

Ingredients

> Eggplant – 500 grams
> Red chilli powder – 1 teaspoon
> Turmeric powder – ½ teaspoon
> Cumin-coriander powder – 1 teaspoon
> Asafoetida – ¼ teaspoon
> Rice flour – 1 tablespoon
> Chickpea flour – 1 tablespoon
> Salt to taste
> Oil for frying

Method

In a bowl, mix together red chilli powder, turmeric, cumin-coriander powder, asafoetida, rice flour, chickpea flour and salt.

Chose a large-sized purple eggplant. Wash and pat dry and cut into roundels; rub on both sides with the prepared powdered masala. Heat oil in a non-stick pan and add the eggplant roundels. Fry on a medium flame, flip till they are crisp from outside and soft within. Remove with a slotted spoon and drain. This can be served as an accompaniment with most meals.

Optional: Garnish with sesame seeds.

Rice Recipes

Coconut Rice

The Bene Israel Jews have a preference for coconut rice, known as narieli bhaat.

Ingredients

    Long-grained or Basmati rice – 2 ½ cups
    Saffron – 4 to 5 strands
    Cinnamon stick – 1 medium
    Cloves – 3–4
    Cardamom – 3–4
    Bay leaf – 1
    Onion – 1 small
    Coconut milk – 2 ½ cups
    Turmeric powder – ½ teaspoon
    Water – 2 ½ cups
    Salt to taste

Method

Soak the long-grained rice or Basmati rice in water. Separately, in a small bowl of warm water, soak saffron and keep aside. Heat oil in a vessel and temper with whole spices – cinnamon stick, cloves, crushed cardamoms and bay leaf. Add sliced onions and brown. The rice is then added in with water, coconut milk, turmeric powder, salt and the saffron water. Mix the ingredients and cover the vessel with a lid and cooked on a low flame. When the aroma of the coconut rice will fill the house, it's done. Remove the vessel from the stove. The coconut rice can be served with a curry.

Biryani

Ingredients

- Chicken – 500 grams
- Oil – ½ cup
- Basmati rice – 500 grams
- Cashew nuts – 50 grams
- Bay leaf – 4
- Cinnamon – 1 stick
- Cloves – 3
- Black peppercorns – 4
- Big black cardamoms – 2
- Small cardamoms – 2
- Star anise – 2
- Onions – 3
- Ginger-garlic paste – 2 tablespoons
- Red chilli powder – 1 tablespoon
- Turmeric powder – 1 teaspoon
- Garam masala – 1 tablespoon
- Cumin-coriander powder – 1 tablespoon
- Potato – 1
- Lemon – 1
- Coriander leaves – ¼ cup
- Salt to taste

Method

Wash the chicken pieces. Heat oil in a vessel, slice and fry 1 onion till brown and remove with a slotted spoon onto a plate. Keep it aside along with a few fried cashew nuts for garnishing. Slice 2 more onions and fry in the same vessel with bay leaf, star anise, ginger-garlic paste and whole garam masala. Add the chicken and cook on a low flame. Add red chilli powder, turmeric, coriander-cumin with garam masala. Mix, stir and add 2 glasses of water. Cook the chicken on a medium flame till tender. Add peeled, cubed potato pieces and lemon juice, stir and cover with a lid.

Simultaneously, wash the rice, soak in warm water for half an hour, wash, strain and keep aside. When the chicken is almost done, reduce the flame, spread rice over chicken, cover with a lid and cook for twenty minutes till the rice is soft. Take off the lid, garnish with fried cashew nuts, fried onions, coriander leaves and remove vessel from stove. Again, cover vessel with the lid for fifteen more minutes, as the fragrance of biryani fills the house with its aromatic flavours.

Serve the biryani with a long-handled steel spatula, along with a mixed salad of onion rings, slivers of carrots, chopped tomatoes and boiled-peeled-cubed-beetroot mixed with lemon juice.

Optional: Strands of saffron dissolved in a bowl of warm water can be added when the biryani is garnished with fried onions and cashew nuts.

Note: Indian Jews make biryani during most festivals. Vegetable biryani is also made in the same manner, but with peas, potatoes, carrots and fresh beans. It is garnished with boiled baby potatoes, chopped nuts and crisp fried onions.

Khichdi

For most Indians, khichdi is comfort food. The Bene Israel Jews make moong dal khichdi the same way as it is everywhere else in India. It is often served with bombil. The khichdi-and-bombil combination is often made for Shabbath, as it cooks quickly when Shabbath ends on Saturday evening.

Rice Chapattis or Tandlya-chi-bhakhri

Ingredients

 Rice flour – 2 cups
 Water – 2 cups
 Oil – 1 tablespoon
 Salt to taste

Method

In a vessel, boil water with ½ teaspoon oil and ½ teaspoon salt. Mix, stir, add rice flour, break lumps with a wooden spatula. Simmer on a low flame while stirring continuously. Remove vessel from stove, transfer mixture onto a platter while still warm and knead the dough with greased palms. Divide the dough into small balls, roll into chapattis and roast lightly on a griddle. Flip, serve hot or store in a chapatti box.

 Note: Rice chapattis are often served with mutton curry during Passover.

Sol Kadhi

Ingredients

 Coconut milk – 5 cups
 Rice powder – 1 tablespoon
 Cocum petals – 4
 Red chilli powder – 1 teaspoon
 Turmeric – ½ teaspoon
 Cumin – 1 teaspoon
 Water – 1 cup
 Salt to taste
 (Optional: Garlic – 1 clove; Green chilli –1)

Method

Mix coconut milk in a vessel with salt, powdered chilli, turmeric and cumin. Soak cocum petals in a bowl of water for five minutes, wash and add to the coconut milk. In a small bowl, soak powdered rice in water for ten minutes and add to the coconut milk. Cook the sol kadhi on a low flame and stir continuously till it has a pleasing pink colour. It is served by itself or with rice.

Optional: Slit green chillies can be added in with a diced clove of garlic.

Note: Cocum petals can also be soaked in water, strained, mixed with coconut milk and salt, processed in a mixer, strained, chilled and served as a cool drink.

Soups

The Bene Israel Jews make soups by boiling meat or chicken pieces with finely chopped onions, diced ginger, whole pieces of cinnamon, cloves, cardamom, garam masala powder and salt. When the water is reduced to half, the soup is removed from the stove and served in soup bowls. For Bene Israel Jews, these soups are a good home remedy to cure colds. They are usually made during winter months.

Desserts

Chik-cha-halva

Ingredients

    Wheat extract or chik – 2 cups

    Water – 1 litre

    Sugar – 4 cups

    Coconut milk – 7 to 8 cups

Cardamom – 2 teaspoons

Nutmeg – ½ teaspoon

Powdered China grass or agar-agar – 3 tablespoons

Almonds – 3½ tablespoons

Pistachios – 3½ tablespoons

Raisins – 2 tablespoons

Vanilla essence – 1 teaspoon

Edible colour – ¼ teaspoon or few drops

Salt – ¼ teaspoon

Method

To make the chik, soak whole wheat in water for three days till the grain puffs up. Process the wheat into a smooth paste, strain, spread out on thalis or a piece of cloth. Then break into pieces and store in jars. Readymade wheat extract or chik is also available in specialty shops in Mumbai.

To make the halva, fill water in a vessel, soak the chik and break lumps with a hand masher. Let it stand for an hour and a half, as the wheat extract settles at the bottom of vessel, and discard the water which surfaces.

Fill a deep vessel with 7 to 8 cups of coconut milk. Mix 2 cups of wheat extract with 4 cups of sugar into it. Cook on a low flame, stirring continuously for five hours till it thickens. Dissolve China grass powder in cold water and add to the halva along with vanilla essence and edible rose-pink colour. Stir continuously while cooking on a low flame, till the halva leaves the sides of the pan. Remove the halva from stove, spread on lightly greased thalis, cool and cut into diamond-shapes. Garnish with finely chopped nuts and cover with an embroidered ceremonial textile.

Halva is served during the Jewish New Year before dinner and again after dinner, as dessert. It has to be eaten fresh as it does not stay for more than two days.

Chik-cha-halva

Sweet Flatbread or Puran Poli

This sweetbread is made by the Bene Israel Jews during Purim.

Ingredients

Chana dal or yellow split peas – 1 cup

Wheat flour – 2 cups

Jaggery – 1 cup

Nutmeg – ¼ teaspoon

Cardamom powder – 1 teaspoon

Oil – 1 tablespoon

Ghee – ½ cup

Rice flour for dusting

Water to mix dough

Method

Wash chana dal or yellow split peas, pressure-cook, cool, mash and then place in a heavy-bottomed kadhai. Mix with an equal amount of sugar and cook on a low flame, stirring continuously till the mixture becomes paste-like and dry. When the mixture is cool, add a small amount of grated nutmeg and crushed cardamom seeds and mix well with the paste. In a separate utensil, mix wheat flour with water and a little oil and knead till it is soft in consistency to make a dough. This dough is covered with a thin muslin cloth and allowed to stand for an hour. Make small balls out of the dough and roll on a board with a rolling pin into puris. Place the chana-dal filling in the centre of each puri, and pinch and close the dough. Dust the filled puris with rice flour and roll on a board with a rolling pin. Fry lightly with ghee on a heavy griddle and serve with vegetarian meals or dal or a bowl of sweetened milk or coconut milk or just with a dollop of ghee.

Kippur-chi-puri or Sweet Puris

Bene Israeli Jews break the fast of Yom Kippur or Day of Atonement with black-grape sherbet and these puris, which are served with vegetarian meals, as dairy products are used to make them.

Ingredients

Dough

Refined flour – 250 grams

Semolina – 250 grams

Corn flour – 50 grams

Butter – 500 grams

Milk – ¼ cup

Water

Pinch of salt

Filling

Grated coconut – 400 grams

Butter – 30 to 40 grams

Sugar – 300 grams

Cardamom powder – 2 teaspoons

Nutmeg – ½ teaspoon

Poppy seeds – 1 teaspoon

Almonds – 50 grams

Pistachios – 50 grams

Raisins – 1 tablespoon

Ghee as required for deep frying

Method

Mix refined flour and semolina in a bowl and make a pliable dough with butter or ghee. Set aside for half an hour in a platter. In a small bowl, mix cornflour with 1 tablespoon ghee and make a paste. Divide dough into equal-sized balls.

Place each ball on a board and roll into chapattis with a rolling pin. Lightly spread the cornflour paste evenly on each chapatti. Repeat this process with 5 chapattis and place each on top of the other.

With greased palms, roll chapattis into a cylinder-like scroll and cut into equal-sized balls. Lightly flatten each ball on a board and roll into three-inch diameter puris.

Make the filling by mixing 1 finely grated coconut, sugar, poppy seeds, raisins, finely chopped almonds and pistachios. Place in a pan, pour 1 teaspoon melted butter, cook till dry, remove from stove and cool. Place a tablespoon of filling on one half of the puri, cover with the other half, seal edges and shape the puri into a half moon or place the puri with filling in a crescent-shaped mould.

Remove, seal, crimp edges with a fork and make frilled edges with a puri-cutter.

Heat ghee in a kadhai, deep-fry the puris till the layers open like flaky pastry, drain, cool and store in a container.

Variation: Kippur-chi-puri is also made with a filling of roasted semolina with the above-mentioned ingredients and fried in vegetable oil, so that it can be served with non-vegetarian food.

4

The Cochin Jews

A few years ago, when I was at a conference in New Delhi, a friend showed me a video clip of pastel being prepared by the Cochin Jews of Kerala. This is what inspired me to travel to the region to interview the Cochin Jews.

Cochin is now known as Kochi. It is a major port on the Malabar Coast of the Arabian Sea. It is surrounded by waterbodies and the land is a mixture of lush green environment and beautiful architecture that has Portuguese, Dutch, Christian, Hindu, Jewish and Muslim influences.

There are about twenty-five Jews living in small pockets in Fort Kochi, Mattancherry and Ernakulam, making brave efforts to preserve their Jewish identity, lifestyle and food habits, including following the strict dietary law of kosher.

Kochi features a lush canopy of trees, including banyan, tamarind, coconut, peepal, laburnum and many more, which is the sight I was greeted by when I visited in the summer. The mango trees were heavy with fruit at the time, as were the the jackfruit trees that almost resembled the sculpture of the Egyptian Goddess Artemis. One could walk in the shaded canopies of banyan, tamarind, raintree, coconut, peepal and so many other trees as bright yellow laburnum flowers cascaded down.

I visited the spectacular Paradesi Synagogue in Fort Kochi, which is a popular tourist attraction, known for its impressive clock tower.

Inside the temple, the ner-tamid or the 'eternal light' lamp is placed in an ancient glassholder. There is an array of old and new chandeliers and glass lamps in the synagogue. It is decorated with blue tiles from China in similar but alternating designs and has an intricately carved wooden ceiling, painted in bright colours and embellished with floral designs and geometric patterns. There is a circular stairway leading to the women's gallery, which is no longer used. Outside and around the synagogue, there are prominent signages of Jew Town, Synagogue Street, spice shops and antique warehouses amidst old Jewish homes with railings and grill windows that bear designs of the Star of David. Sara Cohen, one of the oldest Jews of this small community who passed away in 2019, used to sit at the window of her home, watching tourists as her craftsperson embroidered hamotzi covers, kippas, sacred Jewish textiles and other ritualistic objects, which were on display in the foyer. Sara would also keep a watch on her kitchen as her cook made traditional Jewish dishes, which she had taught her when she was in good health.

In Kochi's Jew Town on Synagogue Street, near the Paradesi Synagogue, there is a strong fragrance of various spices, as this area is known for its spice shops. Long ago, Kerala had attracted traders and travellers as it had an abundance of spices, especially black pepper. The spice shops today are fragrant with cardamom, cinnamon, cloves and various masala powders. When the Jewish community lived in large numbers in Kerala, they incorporated many of these spices in their cuisine.

In another antique warehouse, a tall Jewish Hanukkah stand was displayed, along with other bronze and brass items such as oil lamps, painted wood figurines and masks. In one of the spice shops, an enormous traditional bronze cooking vessel, known as an uruli, was displayed at its entrance. It is supposed to be one of the biggest urulis of the region. They are circular, squat, wide-mouthed vessels available in many sizes. The smaller ones are used for small portions or family cooking and the bigger ones are used for community dinners.

It is possible that when the Cochin Jews settled in Kerala, they cooked in such enormous urulis for weddings, bar mitzvahs and community dinners and used the smaller ones in their own kitchens.

Nearby, at the centre for performing arts, every evening, there are Kathakali performances. The dancers enact the Indian epics, dressed in elaborate costumes, wearing huge circular crowns and imitation gold jewellery, with their faces painted in bright green, blue or pink colours, robust hands moving in mudras with long nails coloured in silver, eyebrows shaped like quivering bows, as their facial muscles express various emotions. The dancers' heavily painted expressive eyes speak volumes as their graceful bodies move to the drumbeats.

A little ahead, Chinese fishing nets are held in place with stone weights.

Later, to reach Ernakulam, we took a boat from a jetty on the seashore at Fort Kochi. The entire evening had a magical feeling, as seagulls and other birds circled above while the fish got caught in the Chinese nets. Hidden amidst the trees, along the seashore, there were birds like coppersmith barbets and green bee-eaters. We watched in amazement as the vibrant blue of a kingfisher's wing stood out against the evening sky, amidst the cargo ships anchored along the coastline with the sound of their horns and flickering lights.

We were told that if lucky, we could even see dolphins doing somersaults in the sea!

If Fort Kochi attracts tourists, Ernakulam in contrast is a rather urban settlement, with high-rises, malls and religious places of all communities. Men are seen wearing the traditional sarong-like mundu, while the women are dressed in beautiful Kerala saris, which are white with dazzling gold borders. Some Jews also wear this attire. The district has plenty of grocery shops, vegetable vendors, fruit stalls, butcher shops, flower shops and bakeries with a rich array of breads, cakes and biscuits. It also has plenty of utensil shops and jewellery shops. Most shops have long strings of chilli-peppers tied on their doorways, maybe to ward off the evil eye. These chillis also make a spicy accompaniment to food when stuffed with a filling of boiled potatoes, which are mashed, mixed with fried onions, red chilli powder, cumin and salt, then dipped in a batter of refined flour and deep fried.

My first stop was at Market Road in Ernakulam to see the synagogue. Here, I met Elias Joseph Hai, who is the managing trustee of Kadavumbagam Synagogue. For years, he has been preserving the synagogue, its history and heritage. Elias and his wife Ofera have an aquarium and nursery of plants at the entrance of the synagogue. At the synagogue, I saw the most luxuriant mango tree; its branches were almost touching the ground. It was in full bloom with fragrant blossoms and huge raw mangoes, which would soon transform into golden-yellow fruit. With pride, Ofera said, 'This particular tree blossoms twice a year.' People of all communities were walking around in the foyer of the synagogue at the time, either buying aquariums or exotic fish, or just watching the fish on display. When I met Elias and his wife, they had bought the eggs of the mullet fish to make a meal of fish-egg pastel, pomfret for meen pollichathu, along with lentil curry and rice. At the end of the week, they were planning to celebrate the Jewish festival of Purim with boli, a sweet flatbread.

The Cochin Jews were known to have come to India before the Christian era. Perhaps it was the exodus from Persia after the destruction of the Second Temple which brought them to Kerala. It is also believed that some more Jews came to Kerala from Spain.

Before the Christian era and afterwards, many travellers had noted the presence of Jews in Cochin. They described it as a Jewish kingdom of India. It is said that the Jews lived here in peace with many communities. In 1686, the Jewish Dutch traveller Moses de Pavia noted the presence of 'Malabaree Jews' in Cochin. They were Jewish in every way and had their own synagogues.

During those difficult days the Zamorin of Calicut and the Portuguese took over the flourishing pepper and spice trade of the Jews. The Raja of Cochin had always respected the Jews and admired their integrity. He granted them the area of Mattancherry, next to the royal temple. He even gave special permission to his Jewish soldiers to observe the Shabbath. For this compassionate gesture, he was known as the King of Jews. This is how Jew Town came into being. The Jewish merchants were prosperous spice traders and had documents about the spice trade, historical background about their arrival in Cochin and precious religious artifacts. Yet, the Zamorim and the Portuguese were a constant cause of worry. With their sudden raids to take over their spice trade, the Jews lost some of their most important documents and artefacts. It was only when the Dutch came to their rescue that they could live in peace. The Dutch merchants protected them, as the Jews were associated with their company. The Dutch East India Company helped them reconstruct the edicts of their religion. When the Jews of Denmark received information about the Cochin Jews, they also helped by providing them with books and religious artefacts.

The Jews built the first synagogue in Cochin. They had a Sefer Torah in a silver steepled casket with delicate engravings, geometric designs and tassels. The parchment of the Sefer Torah was inscribed by hand with squid ink. The texts of the first five books of the Old Testament were inscribed in Hebrew by hand on parchment. During this period (around the year 1568) there were Malabari Jews and Paradesi Jews in Kerala. Through the years, various Jewish communities had come to settle in Kochi and were known as Malabari Jews. They lived in Ernakulam, Mala, Parur, Chendamangalam and Kochi. There were synagogues in Parur and Chendamangalam, which are now in a dilapidated condition. It is said that the Paradesi Jews were descendants of European or Spanish Jews, who came to India in the fifteenth century. They settled in Mattancherry, Kochi, and were known as white Paradesi Jews.

According to scholars, the differences between the Paradesi and Malabari Jews diminished in the twentieth century, and the Jews who made Kerala their home came to be known as Cochin Jews or the Cochinim.

From ancient times, the Malabar spice trade was controlled by the Mattancherry Jewish community of Kerala. Mattancherry is where the Paradesi synagogue is situated and is known as a trade centre for tea and spices. As mentioned earlier, when the Portuguese traders attacked the Cochin Jews to take over the spice trade, it was the only incident of conflict in the history of Indian Jews. Indian Jews have never faced persecution in India.

The Cochin Jews were well-known spice traders, so naturally, they used the same in their cuisine, including black pepper, cardamom, cinnamon, ginger, turmeric, asafoetida, red chillies, green chillies, coriander, cumin, fenugreek seeds, nutmeg, mace, etc., which are some of the indigenous flavours of Kerala. They started using curry leaves, tamarind juice and coconut milk, along with a variety of bananas and chillies. The chillies available to them vary in colour and intensity, and they are chopped, roasted or fried before being added as a tempering to some of the Cochin Jews' recipes.

Earlier, for Shabbath, the Jews of Kochi used to make pita bread or hamotzi or flatbread on a griddle. It is no longer so, as today they use bread bought from a bakery. Sometimes, Jewish women bake their own plaited challah bread in an oven.

In most Jewish homes, the Shabbath bread is covered with a ceremonial cloth. Earlier, Jewish women made these covers themselves, but now they receive them as gifts from Israel, along with Hanukkah candlestands and skullcaps known as kippas or yarmulkes.

The Kerala coastline gives the Cochin Jews easy access to seafood, which they cook according to the Jewish dietary law. But with vegetarian food they use dairy products, even having Indian sweets that are made with milk. The staple diet of the Cochin Jews is varied, including fish curry, rice, chicken curry, meat dishes and the delicious combination of stew with appams, as well as sambhar – made with toor dal or pigeon peas and vegetables, chutney and payasam. They also have a preference for the traditional vegetarian meal of Kerala, known as sadhya, which is a variety of vegetable dishes placed in bowls on a steel thali or plaintain leaf. Most of the Cochin Jews' recipes are made with coconut oil or sunflower oil. They also make regional dishes like idli, vada and dosa. Yet they retain a Jewish lifestyle.

The Cochin Jews also consume one of the most popular fruits grown in Kerala, which is the banana. Many types of bananas are cultivated in Kerala. In fruit shops, bananas are artistically displayed, still attached to their stalks. The Jews of Kochi usually eat bananas at the end of a meal, along with other fruits. Banana chips, tapioca chips and jackfruit chips are served as snacks.

For staples, the Cochin Jews prefer unpolished or par-boiled rice like sona masoori, Basmati or kolam. These are made into many different recipes, which are had for breakfast, lunch and dinner. Dosa, idli, appam, puttu and other recipes are made with rice flour. Coconut rice is also made with finely shredded pieces of coconut, flavoured with cumin seeds and cooked in coconut milk. Most vegetarian meals are served with yogurt or tall glasses of buttermilk. Jews do not have buttermilk with meat dishes, in order to follow the Jewish dietary law. Both vegetarian and non-vegetarian dishes are sometimes served with pickles or fried rice-flour poppadams.

The Jews of Kochi may not have a hazzan or rabbi to hold regular prayers or a mohel to circumcise a male child, but sometimes, if there is a minyan of ten male Jews at the Paradesi synagogue, Shabbath prayers are held. In 2019, the Kadavumbagan Synagogue was renovated with brightly painted wood carvings, embroidered tapesteries and magnificent chandeliers, which give a divine glow to the synagogue.

The Cochin Jews pray in Hebrew, but speak English, Malayalam and other regional languages.

FESTIVALS AND OCCASIONS

Shabbath

On Friday evening, the Cochin Jews make either kubbah (recipe on page 67–68) or pastel (recipe on pages 63-65) or pulao or biryani or potato pattice. Candles are lit and in the absence of challah bread, they buy bread from a bakery or make appams with rice flour. Some women bake challah bread at home and fill a goblet of homemade grape juice for the Kiddush prayers. Often, the Shabbath dinner of the Cochin Jews includes a fish dish known as meen pollichathu (recipe on pages 69-70).

Those Jews who have full-time salaried jobs cannot stop working on the Shabbath, but Jewish traders with private businesses stop work from Friday evening to Saturday evening.

Shabbath Candles

Rosh Hashanah

The Jewish New Year is celebrated with roast chicken or biryani or kubbah. Sometimes, semolina cake or payasam is made with coconut milk. In the absence of kosher wine in India, homemade grape wine is used in most Jewish homes.

Yom Kippur

The Day of Atonement is observed by praying and fasting. A wheat-flour halva is made to break the fast of Yom Kippur (recipe on page 92–93).

Passover

As with all Jewish communities, the story of the Exodus from Egypt is read during Passover. It is a constant source of inspiration for Jews all over the world. A traditional Passover table or Seder is set with a ritualistic meal. During Passover, most Jewish households ensure that all utensils are washed in warm water, in adherence with the dietary law. Passover is celebrated at home or in a rented hall, where tables are arranged, covered with clean tablecloths, upon which candles are lit. Platters are prepared for the Passover Seder with symbolic ingredients like lettuce, which is used as maror or bitter herbs. Celery or parsley stalks are placed as karpas on the platter, along with a bowl of salt water or lemon juice or vinegar, to signify sorrow. Haroset is made to signify the mortar used by the Jews when they built the Pyramids. Beitzah or a boiled egg is placed with jerova or zeroa, the roasted shankbone, which is symbolic of the sacrificial lamb. Often, the wing of a roasted chicken is also placed in the Seder platter. A special table with a Seder platter is prepared for an elder who leads the prayers.

Purim

A sweet flatbread known as boli is made to celebrate the liberation of Persian Jews (recipe on page 93).

Sukkot

A tent is constructed in the courtyard of a synagogue, as Sukkot is observed by dwelling in tents. It is symbolic of the forty years of wandering before the Jews returned to Israel. Cochin Jews make hubba or pastel with coconut pulao for Sukkot.

Shavout

When there was a large community of Cochin Jews in Kerala, they made small, sweet rice balls. These were showered on the congregation at the synagogue from the women's gallery during Shavout to celebrate the time when Prophet Moses received the Ten Commandments.

Sukkot

This festival marks the completion of reading the Torah. The Cochin Jews make a festive meal with kubbah and pastel to celebrate it.

Hanukkah

Candles are lit to celebrate Hanukkah, and cutlets and potato pakoras are served along with a variety of fried snacks.

Tisha B'Av

Most Jews fast during Tisha B'Av, which is observed in memory of the fall of the Second Temple. In Kerala, this fast is broken with rice-flour sweets (recipe on page 91).

RECIPES

Grape Juice

In India, most Jewish festivals are incomplete without grape juice (recipe on page 24).

Pastel

This is an unusual recipe made only by the Jews of Cochin. The pastel is shaped like a half moon, a croissant or a roll.

Ingredients

Dough
Refined flour – 2 cups
Coconut milk – ¼ cup
Vegetable oil – ¼ cup
Eggs – 2

Salt to taste

Water as needed

Filling

Vegetable oil – 4 cups

Chicken mince – 1 cup

Coconut milk – ¼ cup

Onion – 1

Ginger-garlic paste – 1 tablespoon

Green chillies – 2

Turmeric powder – ¼ cup

Black pepper powder – ¼ teaspoon

Cinnamon – 1 ½ inch stick

Lemon juice – ½ teaspoon

Coriander leaves – 2 tablespoons

Mint leaves – 3

Water as needed

Salt to taste

Method

In a bowl, break 1 egg, whisk and mix with flour, salt, vegetable oil, cinnamon powder and coconut milk. Knead into a dough with ¼ cup water. Cover with a damp cloth and let stand for fifteen minutes.

Heat oil in a deep pan and add finely chopped onions, grated ginger, diced garlic, chopped green chillies, salt, powdered turmeric and black pepper and keep aside.

Wash the chicken mince in a vessel, add water and cook till tender.

Heat oil in another pan, fry finely chopped onions, add ginger-garlic paste, finely diced chillies, salt, powdered turmeric and black pepper. Then add the chicken mince, mix, stir and cook on a low flame till dry. When cool, add the lemon juice, the finely chopped coriander leaves with mint leaves and keep aside.

Divide the dough prepared earlier into lemon-sized balls and roll 2½ inch-diameter puris on a board with rolling pin. Place a tablespoon of the chicken-mince mixture in the centre of each puri and seal. Shape it into a crescent and keep aside.

In another bowl, whisk an egg and brush the pastel crescents with the egg wash. Repeat the process on each crescent. Heat oil in a kadhai, fry the pastels till they puff up. Remove with a slotted spoon onto a platter and serve.

Variation: Pastel can be made with shredded chicken or chicken mince mixed with two or more ingredients, such as mashed potatoes, grated boiled eggs, juliennes of cabbage, carrots and capsicum, or steam-cooked and mashed fish eggs.

Pastel

Pastillas

These are similar to mini chicken pies.

Ingredients

Chicken pieces – 500 grams
Onions – 2
Eggs – 2
Black pepper – 1 tablespoon
Ginger – 1 tablespoon

Cinnamon powder – ½ teaspoon
Almonds – 1 tablespoon
Coriander leaves – 2 tablespoons
Oil – 2 cups
Salt to taste
Half a lime
Refined flour – 2 cups
Water – as needed

Method

Boil chicken pieces in water on a high flame for twenty-five minutes till chicken is cooked. Remove the chicken pieces from the water and keep the stock aside. Place chicken pieces on a chopping board and cut into smaller pieces.

Heat oil in a pan and fry the sliced onions till they are golden brown. Crack and beat the eggs, then add to the chicken stock and mix in black pepper, finely chopped ginger, cinnamon powder, coarsely chopped almonds, chicken pieces, chopped coriander leaves, a squeeze of lime and salt. Cook for eight minutes and keep aside to cool.

Remove chicken mixture from stock with a slotted spoon, drain, place on a plate, dry and use as a filling.

To make the pastilla cover, cut filo sheets into rectangular strips. If filo sheets are not available, the covering can made with refined flour dough (mixing refined flour and water to make a dough). The dough is cut into balls, placed on a board, rolled with a rolling pin into a chapatti and cut into strips. Oil is applied to each strip, then the chicken mixture is placed within. The strips are shaped into rectangular packages and brushed with egg wash, placed on grease-proof paper or an oiled tray, then baked in an oven or shallow fried in a pan till they are crisp.

Kubbah

Kubbah is made with refined-flour or rice-flour dough and salt, with a minced meat or chicken filling inside.

Ingredients

Dough
Refined flour or rice flour – 2 cups
Salt – ½ teaspoon
Water – 1 cup

Filling
Finely chopped onion – ½ cups
Shredded chicken or minced meat or fish – 250 grams
Salt, pepper and cumin to taste

Soup
Oil – 1 tablespoon
Onion – 1
Potatoes or sweet potatoes – 2
Zucchini – 1
Carrot – 1
Celery – ¼ cup
Turmeric powder – 1 teaspoon
Water – 7 cups
Salt to taste

Method

Mix flour and salt with water to prepare a dough. Cut the dough into balls, place on a board and roll into puris with a rolling pin.

To make the filling, boil and mash the fish/ minced meat/ chicken and combine with chopped onion, salt, pepper and cumin. Place this mixture in the centre of the puri. Seal the edges around the filling and roll into a round shape like a dumpling and keep aside.

In the meantime, make the soup for the kubbah. Heat oil in a pan, in which sliced onions are lightly browned with diced ginger, cubed potatoes or sweet potatoes, carrots, zucchini, diced celery, turmeric powder and salt. Add the stock used for the filling earlier and water and mix well. Boil on a high flame for five minutes. As the vegetables soften, add the dumplings, garnish with chopped coriander and mint leaves, then cook on medium to low heat for five to ten minutes and serve hot with pulao or rice.

Variation: Sometimes chopped boiled eggs are added to the filling. Pumpkin, okra or beetroot are often added to the kubbah soup as well, along with tamarind juice.

Fish Recipes

According to the dietary law, only fish which have scales are to be cooked. The Cochin Jews' recipe for fried fish is prepared in a particular way. The fish is cleaned, washed, then marinated in red chilli powder, black pepper and salt for ten minutes and deep fried in oil, till it is golden-brown in colour.

Fried Fish

Mullet eggs are also used to make a filling for kubbah dumplings (see pages 68–69).

Another simple recipe is made with sardines. Sardines are marinated in salt, lime juice, crushed garlic and red chilli powder as per quantity for five to ten minutes. They are then grilled and served as a snack with drinks.

Meen Pollichathu or Green Fish Curry

Ingredients

Fish pieces – 500 grams

Oil – 1 ½ tablespoons

Mustard seeds – 1 teaspoon

Coconut milk – 1 ½ cups

Onion – 1

Shallots – 3

Ginger – 1 inch

Garlic – 3 cloves

Green chillies – 3

Cardamom pods – 3

Coriander powder – ½ teaspoon

Garam masala – ½ teaspoon

Black pepper powder – ½ teaspoon

Curry leaves – 7

Fresh coriander leaves – 1 small bouquet

Lemon juice – ½ lemon

Salt to taste

Method

Process the finely chopped onion, ginger, garlic, coriander leaves with half a cup of coconut milk and keep aside.

Heat oil in a casserole, add mustard seeds, curry leaves, crushed cardamom pods, shallots and simmer on a low flame. Add the processed masala prepared above along with finely diced green chillies, black pepper powder, garam masala, salt and ¼ cup water. Cover with a lid and cook on a medium flame for four minutes. Remove lid and add fish pieces, stir, cook on a low flame for three minutes and add one glass of coconut milk. Spoon the masala over the fish and cook on a medium flame for five minutes till the fish is cooked and the gravy thickens. Remove from stove and serve with rice.

Optional: Add one tablespoon pureed tomato along with a tablespoon of tamarind pulp and ¼ teaspoon red chilli powder before the fish is added to the gravy.

Variation: Chicken can be prepared with the same recipe but cook for thirty-five minutes.

Note: This curry is made during Passover.

Meen Unda Kari or Cochin Jewish Fish Kofta Curry

Ingredients

Fish fillets – 500 grams

Oil – 2 tablespoons

Rice flour – 1 tablespoon

Fish masala – 1 tablespoon

Mustard seeds – 1 teaspoon

Fennel seeds – 1 teaspoon

Onion – 1

Cinnamon – 1 medium-sized stick

Ginger-garlic paste – 1 ½ teaspoons

Green chillies – 1

Turmeric powder – ½ teaspoon

Red chilli powder – 1 teaspoon

Cumin powder – 1 teaspoon

Cardamom – ¼ teaspoon

Black pepper – ½ teaspoon

Sugar – 1 teaspoon

Tamarind juice – 1 teaspoon

Refined flour – 1 tablespoon

Fresh coriander leaves – 1 small bouquet

Salt to taste

Method

Clean and wash fish fillets and fry lightly in oil for five minutes. Remove, cool and flake by hand. Mix flakes well with fish masala, rice powder, refined flour and salt. Make a kind of dough of this mixture by adding water and kneading, cut into portions, shape into lemon-sized balls and keep aside on a plate.

Heat oil in a kadhai and fry these fish balls till they are golden brown. Then remove with a slotted spoon and keep aside.

For the curry, heat oil in another vessel, in which mustard seeds and fennel seeds are tempered. Add finely chopped onions and brown. To this, add cinnamon stick, ginger-garlic paste, chopped green chillies, fish masala, turmeric powder, red chilli powder, cumin powder, cardamom, black pepper, finely chopped coriander leaves, sugar, tamarind juice and salt. Next, mix a slurry of refined flour and rice flour with the curry. Add the fried fish balls to the curry and cook on a low flame till the sauce thickens, after which garnish with chopped coriander leaves. The curry is served hot with rice.

Chicken and Egg Recipes

Chicken in Coconut Curry

Ingredients

    Chicken pieces – 500 grams
    Coconut oil – ½ cup
    Coconut milk – 1 glass
    Onion – 1 large
    Ginger-garlic paste – 1 tablespoon
    Curry leaves – 10
    Green chillies – 2
    Red chilli powder – 1 teaspoon
    Turmeric powder – ½ teaspoon
    Cumin powder – 1 teaspoon
    Garam masala – 1 teaspoon
    Water – 2 ½ glasses
    Salt to taste

Method

To make this curry, wash and keep aside chicken pieces. Heat coconut oil in a pan, add sliced onions and fry till brown. Add curry leaves, ginger-garlic paste, chopped green chillis, mix well and cook on a low flame for a few minutes. Then add chicken pieces and mix well, add red chilli powder, turmeric and cumin, garam masala, salt and water and cook on a medium flame till the chicken is almost tender. Serve hot with rice.

Chicken Curry with Poppy-seed Paste

Ingredients

Chicken – 500 grams
Oil – ¼ cup
Poppy-seed paste – 2 tablespoons
Coconut milk – 1 glass
Mustard seeds – ¼ teaspoon
Onions – 2
Curry leaves – 6
Ginger-garlic paste – 1 tablespoon
Green chillies – 2
Bay leaf – 1
Cinnamon – 1 medium stick
Cardamoms pods – 2
Black peppercorns – 4
Cloves – 2
Tamarind pulp – 1 tablespoon
Red chilli powder – 2 teaspoons
Turmeric powder – 1 teaspoon
Cumin powder – 1 teaspoon
Coriander powder – 2 teaspoons
Chopped coriander leaves – 2 tablespoons
Salt to taste
Water

Method

Wash chicken pieces. In a small pan, dry-roast poppy seeds, cool, soak in a bowl of water for five minutes, drain and process in a mixer with 4 dry red chillies and ¼ cup water. Make into a paste and remove in a bowl.

Heat oil in a vessel and temper with mustard seeds, curry leaves, bay leaf, cinnamon stick, cloves, black peppercorns, cardamom pods and chopped green chillies. Add finely chopped onions and sauté till transparent. Mix with ginger-garlic paste, salt, red chilli powder, turmeric, cumin and coriander. Add 1 ½ cups of water, mix, stir, simmer on a low flame for five minutes. Add chicken pieces with the poppy-seed paste, stir, cover with a lid. Cook on a medium flame for twenty-five minutes till chicken is tender. Add tamarind pulp and cook for five more minutes on a low flame till the gravy thickens. Garnish with chopped coriander leaves and serve with rice.

Chicken in Cashew Nut Sauce

Ingredients

> Boneless chicken pieces – 500 grams
> Onions – 2
> Ginger-garlic paste – 1 tablespoon
> Tomato puree – 1 cup
> Red chilli powder- 1 teaspoon
> Turmeric – ½ teaspoon
> Cumin – 1 teaspoon
> Cashew nuts – 12
> Salt to taste

Method

To make this recipe, wash boneless chicken pieces and keep aside. Process chopped onions in a mixer with ginger-garlic paste, red chilli powder, turmeric, cumin, cashew nuts and salt to make a masala paste. Heat oil in a vessel and lightly fry the masala paste with tomato puree, then simmer on a low flame. Add cubed chicken pieces to the paste, along with water, after which cover the dish with a lid and cook on a high flame till chicken is cooked. The completed dish is garnished with finely chopped coriander leaves and served hot with rice or bread.

Jewish Fried Chicken

Ingredients

    Chicken – 500 grams
    Ginger-garlic paste – 2 tablespoons
    Turmeric – 1 teaspoon
    Black pepper powder – 1 teaspoon
    Onions – 3
    Curry leaves – 7
    Red chilli powder – 1 teaspoon
    Garam masala – 1 teaspoon
    Green chillies – 2
    Tomatoes – 2
    Vinegar – 1 teaspoon
    Water – 1 glass
    Salt to taste

Method

Cut chicken into medium-sized pieces, mix with ginger-garlic paste, turmeric powder, salt and black pepper and keep aside for two hours. Then heat oil in a pan and fry the chicken pieces and keep aside. In the same pan, add more oil to brown the sliced onions, add curry leaves, slit green chillies, turmeric powder, red chilli powder, garam masala, finely chopped tomatoes, salt, water and vinegar. Cook for seven minutes, add the fried chicken pieces and cook for a few more minutes on a medium flame till the gravy thickens.

Jewish Cutlets

Ingredients

Chicken breasts – 6

Eggs – 2

Breadcrumbs or semolina – 1 cup

Oil – ½ cup, or as needed for frying

Salt – ½ teaspoon per cutlet, plus to taste

Method

To make these cutlets, wash and pat-dry chicken breasts, rub with salt, dip in beaten egg mixture, then cover with breadcrumbs or semolina and keep aside. Heat oil in a pan and deep-fry the chicken cutlets till crisp on both sides, then remove from the pan with a spatula, place in a platter and serve as a one-dish meal or snack or as an accompaniment to gravy-based dishes.

Chicken Soup

Chicken – 500 grams

Water – 5 glasses

Onion – 1 large

Potato – 1 large

Tomatoes – 2

Turmeric powder – 1 teaspoon

Black pepper – 1 ½ teaspoon

Coriander leaves – 1 tablespoon

Salt to taste

Method

Boil water in a heavy-bottomed vessel and add washed pieces of chicken, sliced onions, cubed potatoes, chopped tomatos, powdered turmeric, black pepper, chopped coriander leaves and salt. Boil the soup on a medium flame till the chicken is tender and serve hot in soup bowls.

Chicken Stew

Ingredients

    Chicken – 500 grams

    Oil – 3 tablespoons

    Black peppercorns – 4

    Cinnamon – ½ inch stick

    Cloves – 2

    Cardamom pods – 2

    Bay leaves – 2

    Onion – 1

    Ginger – 1 inch

    Green chillies – 2

    Refined flour – 1 tablespoon

    Potato – 1

    Coconut milk – 2 glasses

    Curry leaves – 10

    Salt to taste

Method

Heat oil in a large casserole and add sliced onion. Sauté till transparent. Add curry leaves, finely chopped ginger and refined flour and keep stirring for a few minutes. Then add bay leaves, cinnamon stick, clove, cardamom pods, peppercorns, slit green chillies and chicken pieces; mix and stir. Add one glass of thin coconut milk and cook on a low flame for twenty minutes. Cover with lid askew and cook till the gravy is reduced to half, then add the peeled and cubed potato and another glass of coconut milk. Cook on a medium flame till the potato is soft and chicken is tender. Cook on a low flame for another five to ten minutes. Garnish with finely chopped coriander leaves, remove from stove and serve hot with appam or rice.

Optional: You can add shallots too.

Variation: A vegetable stew is also made with potatoes, carrots, fresh green beans and shelled peas.

Egg Curry

Ingredients

Eggs – 6

Curry leaves – 5

Cinnamon – 1 medium-sized stick

Fennel seeds – ½ teaspoon

Onions – 2

Tomatoes – 2

Coconut milk – 1 ½ glass

Ginger-garlic paste – 1 tablespoon

Green chillies – 1

Red chilli powder – 1 teaspoon

Cumin powder – 1 teaspoon

Coriander leaves – 1 small bunch

Turmeric – ½ teaspoon

Oil – 2 ½ tablespoon

Water – 1 glass

Salt to taste

Method

To make this curry, shell eggs, boil and keep aside. Heat oil in a vessel and add curry leaves, fennel seeds and cinnamon stick. After this, brown sliced onions with ginger-garlic paste, chopped green chillies, red chilli powder, cumin, coriander, turmeric, black pepper and salt. Add finely chopped tomatoes along with water, mix well and cook till the gravy thickens. Make small gashes on the boiled eggs and add to the curry with the coconut milk and finely chopped coriander leaves. The egg curry is cooked for ten minutes and served hot with rice or bread.

Variation: Cut boiled eggs into halves and add to the curry.

Meat Recipes

Meat Curry

This curry is made during Passover by the Cochin Jews.

Ingredients

Lamb meat – 500 grams

Turmeric powder – 1 teaspoon

Red chilli powder – 1 teaspoon

Black pepper – 1 teaspoon

Coconut milk – 1 cup

Vinegar – ¼ cup

Oil – ½ cup

Big onions – 1

Curry leaves – 7

Ginger-garlic paste – 1 tablespoon

Tomato – 1 large

Dates – 2

Tamarind pulp – 1 teaspoon

Water as needed

Sugar – ½ teaspoon

Salt to taste

Method

Clean, wash and cube meat, then marinate in powdered turmeric, red chilli powder, black pepper and vinegar. Heat oil in a heavy-bottomed vessel, in which sliced onions are browned with curry leaves and ginger-garlic paste. Add cubed meat into the pan and sauté, after which add water with salt and finely chopped tomatoes. Cook for an hour or till the meat is tender and serve with rice.

Variation: Wash meat pieces and cut into strips. Marinate in red chilli powder, turmeric, black pepper and salt. Heat oil in a vessel, fry meat strips and then keep aside. Brown sliced onions in the same oil, adding ginger-garlic paste, boiled and pureed dates, tamarind pulp, coconut milk, powdered turmeric, black pepper, a pinch of sugar, salt and chopped coriander leaves. The curry is simmered on a low flame and meat strips are added and cooked till the sauce thickens.

Minced Meat Cutlets

Ingredients

Minced meat – 500 grams

Garam masala – 1 teaspoon

Onion – 1

Ginger-garlic paste – 1 teaspoon

Green chilli – 1

Potatoes – 7

Breadcrumbs – 1 cup

Eggs – 2

Salt to taste

Method

Boil minced meat, grind to a paste in a stone mortar or process in a mixer, place in a bowl and mix with powdered garam masala and salt. Heat oil in a pan, and brown sliced onions. Add ginger-garlic-green chilli paste and cook. The minced meat is added last, mixed well, then cooled, shaped into cutlets and kept aside.

Before making the cutlets, boil potatoes, peel, mash, mix with salt and keep aside. Flatten small balls of mashed potatoes into puris and place the minced meat filling in the centre. Close, seal and keep aside.

In another bowl, beat eggs and add salt. Keep breadcrumbs on another plate, in which the cutlets are to be rolled.

Dip the mince cutlets in the egg mixture, then roll in the breadcrumbs, shallow fry, flip so as to cook the cutlet on both sides, till the cutlets are crisp and golden brown.

Remove cutlets from the pan with a spatula and serve as a one-dish meal, snack or accompaniment to gravy-based dishes.

Breakfast Recipes

Appam

Appams are made all over Kerala. These are also known as hoppers in some places. The Cochin Jews often make appams for Shabbath prayers.

Ingredients

    Regular white rice – 2 cups
    Parboiled rice or boiled rice or idli rice – 1 cup
    Poha or cooked rice – 1 handful
    Coconut milk – 1 cup or Grated coconut – 1 ½ cups
    Dry active yeast – ½ teaspoon or Toddy – 1 teaspoon
    Sugar – 2 tablespoons
    Water as required for grinding
    Oil as required
    Salt to taste

Method

Rinse both the rice varieties together for a couple of times. Soak both the regular rice and parboiled rice in water for 4 to 5 hours.

Drain and then add them to the grinder. Also add the grated coconut, cooked rice or poha, dry active yeast or toddy, salt and sugar. Add required amount of water and grind all the ingredients into a smooth flowing batter. Pour the batter in a large bowl or pan. Cover and keep aside for fermenting for eight to twelve hours, depending on the temperature conditions.

The batter is fried with oil in an iron griddle or a special appam pan till the centre is soft, but has frilled edges. Appams are served as an accompaniment to stews and curry-based dishes.

Variation: Another kind of appam is the kallappam, which is made on Jewish festive occasions. The batter is made with coarse rice flour, which is fermented in yeast or toddy. This batter is poured with a ladle onto a griddle and spread in a pefect round shape, then roasted till done.

Another dish known as uzhunnu appam is made using idli batter mixed with coconut milk. The batter is poured with a ladle onto a hot griddle and roasted till done.

Puttu

Puttu is often made for breakfast and eaten with egg curry, kadala curry or vegetable stew.

Ingredients

Puttu flour (coarsely ground rice flour) – 1 cup

Water – ⅓ cup for 1 cup flour; increase or decrease as per this ratio

Salt – ⅓ teaspoon or to taste

Fresh grated coconut – ½ cup

Water for steaming – 2 to 3 cups

Method

Put rice flour in a mixing bowl or a pan and add salt. Then add the water, put in a grinder and mix till there are no lumps. It should be a moist flour with crumbly texture. You will need a puttu maker or puttu kudam to make puttu. Pour 2 cups water in the base vessel of the puttu kudam and heat. Layer the cylindrical vessel of the puttu maker with 2 tablespoons of fresh grated coconut, followed by 3 tablespoons of puttu flour right to the top. Close and place inside the base vessel once the water starts to boil. Steam for five minutes or until the steam starts coming out of the puttu maker. Remove the cylindrical vessel from the base and rest for two minutes. The puttu is then removed with a long-handled spoon onto a plate and served hot with a curry or stew.

Earlier, puttu was made in a hollow bamboo. The bamboo would be be filled with the puttu and coconut mix, and the opening on top was sealed with plantain leaves, while the bottom was placed over the steamer.

Vegetarian Recipes

Pulao

Ingredients

    Basmati rice – 1 cup
    Oil – 3 tablespoons
    Onion – 1
    Garlic – 2 cloves
    Turmeric powder – ½ teaspoon
    Garam masala – ½ teaspoon
    Coconut milk – 1½ cups
    Chicken broth – 1 cup
    Raisins – 2 tablespoons
    Cashew nuts – 3 tablespoons
    Water as needed
    Salt to taste

Method

Soak rice in a bowl of water for ten minutes.

Heat oil in a deep vessel and fry chopped onions. Add finely chopped garlic and garam masala and fry till the onions are transparent. Add the rice, stir, add coconut milk, salt, turmeric and chicken broth. Stir and cook on a low flame for fifteen minutes till the rice is soft and has an aromatic flavour. Remove the lid, garnish with raisins and roasted cashew nuts, cover for few minutes, remove from stove and serve hot with chicken curry.

Note: This pulao is made for Simchat Torah.

Kadala Curry

Ingredients

- Bengal brown gram (chickpeas) – 2 cups
- Oil – 2 tablespoons
- Mustard seeds – ½ teaspoon
- Asafoetida – ¼ teaspoon
- Dry red chillies – 2
- Curry leaves – 10
- Onions – 2
- Ginger-garlic paste – 1 tablespoon
- Green chilli – 1
- Tomato – 1
- Coconut milk – ¾ cup
- Chilli powder – ¼ teaspoon
- Coriander powder – 1 tablespoon
- Kerala garam masala powder (ground whole spices) – 1 teaspoon
- Water – 3 glasses
- Salt to taste

Method

Soak Bengal brown gram chana or chickpeas in a vessel of water for ten hours or overnight, covered with a lid. Then drain and wash them. Add water and pressure-cook for thirty minutes, till soft.

Heat oil in a vessel, temper with mustard seeds, curry leaves, asafoetida, 1 dry red chilli and diced green chilli. Add chopped onions, sauté till transparent, add ginger-garlic paste, finely chopped tomatoes, powdered turmeric, 1 red chilli, coriander, garam masala, salt, chickpeas, coconut milk and cook for ten to fifteen minutes on a medium flame till the gravy thickens. Garnish with coriander leaves and serve hot with rice.

Thoran

This recipe can be made with finely chopped cabbage or any other finely chopped vegetables.

Ingredients

Cabbage or any other vegetable – 1 medium

Curry leaves – 10 to 12

Black mustard seeds – 1 teaspoon

Cumin seeds – 1 teaspoon

Green chilli – 1 chopped

Turmeric powder – ½ teaspoon

Grated coconut – ½ cup, fresh or frozen

Coconut oil –1 or 2 tablespoons

Salt to taste

Coriander leaves for garnishing (optional)

Method

Heat the coconut oil in a kadhai, sauté the mustard seeds, cumin seeds, green chillies and curry leaves. Add turmeric powder and then add the vegetable and salt. Stir and saute for a minute or two, then cook on a low flame. After the vegetable is cooked, add the coconut and stir and cook for two or three minutes. Take off the heat and serve. The dish is served as an accompaniment to most meals.

Coconut Chutney

Ingredients

    Grated coconut – 1 cup
    Ginger – ½ inch
    Red chilli powder – 1 teaspoon
    Dry red chillis – 3
    Tamarind pulp – 20 grams
    Salt to taste

Method

Process grated coconut, crushed ginger, red chilli powder, dry red chillies, salt and a small amount of tamarind pulp in a mixer with a drizzle of water. Removed onto a plate, shape into a ball with oil-greased palms and serve in a bowl.

Pachadi

The Cochin Jews have pachadi only with vegetarian dishes, to maintain the dietary law.

Ingredients

    Yogurt – ½ cup
    Cucumber – 1 medium to large
    Ginger – ½ inch
    Mustard seeds – ¼ teaspoon
    Green chilli – 1, chopped
    Dry red chilli – 1
    Curry leaves – 5 to 6
    Salt to taste
    Water as required

Method

To make pachadi, yogurt is mixed with finely diced ginger, salt and cubed Kerala cucumbers, to which is added tempered mustard seeds, chopped green chillies, whole dry red chillies and curry leaves. The dish is served in a bowl as an accompaniment to vegetarian meals.

Variation: As an alternative to cucumber, cleaned and washed pearl onions, cubed pineapple or boiled pieces of pumpkin or beetroot can be added to the pachadi.

Desserts

Payasam or Rice Pudding

The Cochin Jews serve payasam made with coconut milk as dessert with meat dishes. They make the same recipe with milk when they have a vegetarian meal.

Ingredients

    Coconut milk – 4 cups
    Rice – ½ cup
    Sugar – 1 cup or as per taste

Method

Soak rice in water for about an hour and drain. Heat coconut milk and once it starts boiling, add rice and sugar and mix. Cook till the rice turns mushy and soft, stirring occasionally to avoid it burning at the bottom. It can be garnished with powdered cardamom or dry fruits.

Unniyappam

The Cochin Jews make these sweet rice dumplings the day before Yom Kippur, with which they break the fast. This ancient recipe needs a special cast-iron pan known as appakkara, which has small circular moulds.

Ingredients

Rice (Basmati or idli) – 1 cup or 200 grams

Oil – ½ tablespoon

Coconut – 3 tablespoons chopped pieces

Bananas – 2

Black sesame seeds – 1 teaspoon

Sugar or jaggery powder – ½ cup or as per taste

Water – ¼ cup

Cardamom – 3 to 4 pods, powdered

Cumin powder – ½ teaspoon

Dry ginger powder – ½ teaspoon

Baking soda – ¼ teaspoon

Coconut oil or ghee for each mould – ½ to 1 teaspoon

Water for soaking rice

Method

To make unniyappam, wash rice and soak for five hours. Grind it, or process in a mixer, with water, sugar or jaggery and bananas and make into a batter. Mix this batter in a bowl with cardamom powder, sesame seeds and coconut. The batter is placed in a refrigerator for five hours.

Then, grease each mould of the pan with oil or ghee, half-fill with batter, place on a stove and cook for a few minutes till the base is golden. Then flip each unniyappam to cook the other side, till it is golden brown in colour all over.

Achappams

These crunchy, sweet-and-savoury rose-shaped biscuits are made for festive occasions.

Ingredients

Rice flour – 1 cup
Oil – 2 cups
Eggs – 2
Sugar – ½ cup
Coconut milk – 1 cup
Sesame seeds – ½ teaspoon
Salt – ¼ teaspoon

Method

In a large bowl, mix rice flour, sugar, sesame seeds, salt and coconut milk, then fold in whisked eggs to make a thick batter, which is covered and kept aside for fifteen minutes.

Heat oil in a kadhai. Immerse a floral-shaped achappam mould with a handle in hot oil and immediately dip into the batter to cover the mould. Dip the mould into the kadhai again, deep fry, then separate the achappam from mould with a fork, and slip back into the hot oil. Fry till crisp on both sides, remove with a slotted spoon, drain and place on a plate. This process is repeated till batter lasts. After cooling, achappams are stored in an airtight container.

Note: Bene Ephraim Jews also make achappams, which are known as rose biscuits.

Achappams or Rose Biscuits

Rice Flour Sweets

The Cochin Jews make this recipe to break the fast of Tisha B'Av, held in memory of the fall of the Second Temple.

Ingredients

    Rice flour – 2 cups
    Water – 4 cups
    Coconut – 1 cup
    Jaggery – 1 cup
    Banana leaves as needed

Method

These sweets are made with rice flour dough. Mix finely grated coconut with jaggery and keep aside. Boil water in a vessel and add the rice flour till it absorbs the water. When cool, this dough is divided into lemon-sized balls which are rolled into puris. Place a small amount of the coconut-jaggery mixture in the centre of each puri, close, seal, then roll into a medium-sized flatbread, which is placed on a banana leaf. The leaf is folded into a packet and steamed till done.

Meruba

This is a sweet jam-like pickle, made for the blessing of new fruit for the Festival of Trees and sometimes also for Rosh Hashanah. It is made with pears and apples. The fruit is cored, cubed, covered with sugar and placed in the refrigerator or in a cool place overnight. The syrup is drained the next day and the same liquid is used to cook the fruit till it is tender. Rosewater is added to it, and the mixture is cooked for a few more minutes, then cooled and bottled. This recipe is also made with citrus fruits or jackfruit.

Halva

The Cochin Jews make halva to break the fast of Yom Kippur or the Day of Atonement. It is made a day before the fast, with raw wheat, which is soaked in water at night.

Ingredients

    Raw wheat – 500 grams
    Sugar – 500 grams
    Ghee – 2 cups
    Cardamom powder – 1 teaspoon
    Rosewater for taste – ¼ teaspoon
    Almonds and cashew nuts for garnishing – 2 tablespoons

Method

After soaking the wheat overnight, drain the excess water, add sugar and process in a mixer with very little water to make into a smooth paste. Transfer the paste to a vessel, cover with a lid and keep aside for an hour. To make the halva, heat ghee in a pan, and add wheat paste. Cook on a low flame, stirring continuously till the halva thickens and absorbs all the ghee, after which remove from the stove.

When cool, pour it onto a platter, sprinkle with cardamom powder and a drizzle of rose water, then garnish with blanched, chopped almonds and cashew nuts. Cut into diamond shapes, cover with a lid and keep aside. This is often served with vegetarian meals. This halva is also known as ural.

Boli

This is a sweet flatbread made for the Jewish festival of Purim. It is similar to puran poli, which is also made by the Bene Israel Jews during Purim.

Ingredients

All-purpose flour – 2 cups

Chickpeas – 1 cup

Jaggery – 1 cup

Cardamom powder – 1 teaspoon

Ghee – as needed

Pinch of saffron

Method

In a bowl, make a dough using the all-purpose flour and water. Divide the dough into lemon-sized balls, roll into puris and keep aside.

In another pan, mix boiled and mashed chickpeas, jaggery and cardamom powder with a pinch of saffron. Sauté lightly for a few minutes, cool, place in the centre of the puri, seal and roll into a flatbread with a rolling pin. Roast this on a griddle with ghee and serve hot or cold.

Note: As boli is made with ghee, a dairy product, it is served with vegetarian dishes to maintain the Jewish dietary law.

Cochin Jewish Coconut Cake

Ingredients

Semolina – 1 cup
Oil – ¾ cup
Sugar – 1¼ cups
Grated coconut – 1 cup
Coconut milk – 1 cup
Eggs – 2
Almonds – 8
Raisins – 10
Cashew nuts – 8
Cardamom powder – ¼ teaspoon

Method

Heat oil in a pan, add semolina and roast. Remove from stove and cool. Whisk eggs in a bowl, then mix in sugar, coconut milk, grated coconut, chopped nuts, raisins, cardamom powder, roasted semolina and whisk into a thick batter. Pour this batter into a greased tray and bake in a preheated oven for thirty minutes at 180 degrees Celsius. Remove cake from oven, cool, cut into slices. This cake is served on festive occasions.

Note: Most festive meals comprise pulao, pastel and dumplings made of chicken mince mixed with vegetables, which are poached in a spicy-soupy stew.

Cochin Jewish Coconut Cake

5

The Baghdadi Jews of Kolkata

I landed at Kolkata's Netaji Subas Chandra Bose International
Airport and got caught in a traffic jam as my taxi made its way
towards the hotel. I could see old buildings, high-rises and malls.
On the pavements, vendors were selling seasonal fruit, jhal muri –
which is a combination of puffed rice, peanuts and gram mixed with
a drizzle of mustard oil – serving chai in clay pots to those looking
for their daily dose of tea. All around, there were buses, trams, cars,
autorickshaws and, of course, the cycle-rickshaw pullers of Kolkata.

That evening, my friend Dalia Ray came by and accompanied me
to a Jewish bakery, which was owned by a well-known Baghdadi
Jewish family of Kolkata. It continues to make a variety of cakes,
like plum cake, along with biscuits, cheese and cream-based bakery
items, using the same age-old recipes. Their fruit cake is still well
known for its colour, form, texture and taste, and has a shelf-life of
about three months. At the bakery, the manager gave me a detailed

description of how they had retained some of the baking traditions that had been introduced by the original family. He had also planned a surprise for me, gifting me baked challah bread, which was shaped like a flower with fourteen petals and sprinkled with sesame and poppy seeds. I was touched and appreciated his welcome gift.

The next morning, I met Ian Zachariah, a prominent personality of the Baghdadi Jewish community, who is a journalist and also well known in the field of advertising. He gave me detailed information about the cuisine and lifestyle of Kolkata's small Baghdadi Jewish community.

But that was not the end of my gastronomical journey as, at the airport, even as my name was being announced, I made a dash to the famous Kolkata patisserie Flury's counter to buy a chicken pattice...

Earlier, too, I had gone to Kolkata when I was invited to the Kolkata Book Fair. During this trip, I went to a restaurant in Tollygunge that serves typical Bengali food, and also went to the original Flury's. I loved walking in the streets – which are always bustling with activity – browsing through bookshops and looking at the sweet shops' displays, fascinated by the innumerable types of sandesh and their varied designs, from circular to conch shaped to floral. I also visited the Tagore family's Kolkata mansion, Thakur Bari, at Jorasanko, and had a snack at a coffee shop on College Street.

While attending the Kolkata Book Fair in 2005, I was introduced to Ian Zachariah, who took me on a tour to Synagogue Street to see the Magen David Synagogue with its beautifully maintained interior with ornate pillars and stained-glass windows. The synagogue has moveable pews arranged around a central podium or 'Teva,' behind which is the 'Ark,' similar to a decorated wooden cupboard, where the Torah caskets are placed. A satin curtain or 'Hekhal' covers the Ark. We also went to the Neveh Shalom Synagogue and the Beth El Synagogue, which are built in the Indo-Western style, with high ceilings, rows of pews, colourful stained-glass windows and a magnificent Ark. From there, I went to Goddess Kali's temple and, in a smaller street, I saw artisans making idols of Goddess Durga. The next day, I took a boat ride on the Hooghly River. It was a bewitching sight to see the holy River Ganga flowing into a sea, and I slipped into the romantic world of Rabindranath Tagore's literature and Satyajit Ray's cinema.

It is a well known fact that Jews from west Asia, including Baghdad, Syria, Basra, Aden, Iran, Afghanistan and other areas, came to settle in India. They were merchants who were collectively known as Baghdadi Jews. They spoke Arabic – some also dressed like Arabs – but during Jewish festivals, they said their prayers in Hebrew. Over the years, they learnt English, became anglicized in their habits and their dress code changed. The Baghdadi Jews had come to India from Iraq in the late eighteenth century and had first landed in Surat, Gujarat. They had their own cemetery there, which was demarcated by a wall from the cemetery of the Bene Israel Jews. Though both these cemeteries have been demolished, they bear testimony to the presence of the Baghdadi Jews and the Bene Israel Jews in western India. Over time, the Baghdadi Jews left Gujarat and moved to Pune and Mumbai in Maharashtra, then onwards to West Bengal, where they settled in Kolkata for business reasons.

The well-known philanthropic Sassoon family were Baghdadi Jews. They built many educational and medical institutions in Mumbai.

Baghdadi Indian Jewish cooking was influenced by local conditions, vegetables and ingredients, with the use of herbs like coriander, fennel and mint. They also started making dal and added ginger, garlic, chillies, whole spices or powdered garam masala and coconut milk to curries. Desserts were made with coconut milk, as a result of an interaction with Indian cuisine, to maintain the Jewish dietary law. These changes gave Baghdadi cuisine a new identity. Even the fresh fruits and vegetables of Bengal gave an Indian touch to their recipes. As Kolkata was, and still is, a cosmopolitan city, the Baghdadi Jews lived in proximity with Armenians, Parsis, Anglo-Indians, Bengalis and other communities, which lent variety to their cuisine.

When the Baghdadi Jews lived in large numbers in Kolkata, it was noted that their Jewish culture and traditions were family oriented. They organized large family gatherings with elaborate meals and a variety of dishes, which were part of Kolkata's Jewish life.

Every week, for Friday night Shabbath dinners and Saturday lunches, they would make aloo makala, fish curry, hameen, roast chicken or lemon-coriander chicken, and mahasha or stuffed vegetables. These were made in large quantities, so that they always had enough for Shabbath dinner and leftovers for the next day's Shabbath lunch.

It is still the same for the Passover Seder and Rosh Hashanah, when special dishes are prepared by the women of the house. Rice, wheat-flour chapattis and paranthas are also made as an accompaniment to most meals, as are khichdi, pulao, fish pickle and luchis or puris. Chops and cutlets are made with spicy chicken mince, shallow fried and served as a snack with drinks. Often, mustard oil is used as a cooking medium by Baghdadi Jews.

Like most Indian Jewish communities, Baghdadi Jews also end their meal with a bowl of fruit or dessert made with non-dairy products, like agar-agar jelly.

Coffee is served without milk whenever it is had after a meal of meat dishes. Baghdadi Jewish households still maintain separate sets of utensils for dairy and meat. A special set of vessels is kept aside as well for the festival of Passover,

The small Jewish community of Kolkata continues to follow the dietary law. When a large community of Baghdadi Jews lived in Kolkata, a shohet ritually slaughtered permitted meats for them to eat. Now, as there are only a few Jews in Kolkata, often living alone, some have learnt to prepare kosher meat on their own. During Jewish festivals, some families order kosher meat or chicken from Mumbai or have fish and vegetables if they cannot find kosher meat. Nowadays, the Baghdadi Jews do not have a shohet, mohel, hazzan or rabbi, so prayers are conducted by elders whenever there is a minyan of ten men available.

FESTIVALS AND OCCASIONS

Shabbath

When the Jewish population was larger, challah was available at the Jewish bakery in Kolkata for Friday night Shabbath prayers. Flat Arab breads or pita breads were also made by Jewish bakers there. In recent times, prayers are said over a chapatti or bread bought from a bakery. Sometimes challah bread is baked at home by some Jewish families. Shabbath night meals begin with aloo makala and roast chicken, followed by mahashas or stuffed vegetables, pulao and a khatta or sour soup, and end with fruit or non-dairy desserts. Often, palm jaggery in crystal form is served as a dessert.

Most Baghdadi Jews stop work on Friday night till Shabbath ends on Saturday evening. They have leftovers from Friday night dinner for Saturday lunch. A delicious Shabbath dish is hameen. To make hameen, a whole chicken is stuffed with minced chicken and spices, which is then slow-cooked overnight in an oven from Friday onwards, so that it can be had for lunch on Saturday (recipe on page 105–106). Shabbath prayers are said in Hebrew but there are also Hebrew books with English translations available for those who do not read Hebrew. Jewish tourists from Western countries also donate English prayers books to synagogues for their congregation. Generally, most Jewish festivals are celebrated by families in their own homes or with friends.

Grape wine was made for Shabbath by some Baghdadi Jews of Kolkata. It was bottled and labelled 'Sacred Wine Beth El Synagogue Calcutta' till the 1980s and sold to community members. Some households continue to make alcohol-free Shabbath wine with blackcurrants or raisins, while others have commercial or Israeli wines.

Earlier, community dinners were sponsored and organized by the synagogue committee in the courtyard of a synagogue. In recent times, with the decline in the number of Jews, community dinners are arranged or sponsored by some prominent Jews of Kolkata at a rented hall or in the courtyard of a synagogue, if functional.

The staple diet of most Baghdadi Jews is rice, wheat-flour chapattis or refined flour puris (luchis), chicken, fish, vegetables and seasonal fruit. To maintain the dietary law, coconut milk is used to cook meat dishes, as a flavouring for soups or to make homemade sweets. Baghdadi Jews speak English, Hindi and Bengali. Earlier, they used to speak Arabic too.

Rosh Hashanah

The Rosh Hashanah celebrations begin by having apples dipped in honey. The New Year meal is similar to that made for Shabbath.

Apples Dipped in Honey for Rosh Hashanah

Purim

During this festival, gifts of cakes, pastries, baklava, almond sambouseks and halva with fruit preserves are given to friends and relatives.

Passover

Earlier, matzo bread was made by the Baghdadi Jews in the courtyard of the synagogue and distributed to community members. Today, they receive matzo in packed boxes from Jewish organizations in India and abroad. A dates dish called halek is made for Passover as well. The Passover meal is similar to recipes made for Shabbath.

Sukkot

During this festival, a tent is constructed in the courtyard of a synagogue, as Sukkot is observed by dwelling in tents.

Shavout

This festival is celebrated to rejoice the receiving of the Ten Commandments on Mount Sinai. This is a harvest-related festival, so Baghdadi Jews have dairy products such as sambouseks with a filling of cheese (recipe on page 111-112), or pastries.

Hanukkah

This festival of lights is celebrated by lighting candles and making recipes similar to those used for a Shabbath meal, which is served with semolina halva.

RECIPES

Aloo Makala

According to Ian Zachariah, aloo makala is also known as 'jumping potatoes'. This is the culinary pride of Baghdadi Jews. It is made with whole-fried potatoes. These potatoes have to be a little old as old potatoes have reduced amounts of moisture.

Ingredients

> Potatoes – 12
> Water for boiling
> Oil for frying
> Salt to taste

Method

To make aloo makala, peel and wash potatoes and pat dry. Pierce them all over with a fork. Then boil them in a large pot of salted water on a high flame for fifteen minutes till they are partially cooked. Drain, cool and keep aside.

In a deep pan, pack the parboiled potatoes, cover with oil and cook on a medium flame for fifteen minutes, rotating often, till they are covered with a golden crust. Reduce flame, simmer for seven minutes, flip to prevent sticking and remove from stove. Before serving, place the frying pan back on stove and, on a low flame, fry for seven more minutes, till the potatoes are crisp. Serve hot.

Note: With their crisp exteriors and soft cores, these potatoes have to be cut with precision or they have a tendency to 'jump' off the plate, therefore they are also known as 'jumping potatoes'.

Aloo Makala

Sauces

Hilbe or Hulba

Ingredients

    Fenugreek seeds – 1 tablespoon
    Hot water – 1 cup
    Coriander leaves – 1 cup
    Garlic cloves – 3
    Green chilli – 1
    Ginger – 1 ½ inch ginger
    Lemon juice – ¾ teaspoon
    Salt to taste

Method

Soak fenugreek seeds in warm water for two hours. Drain, mix with salt, fresh coriander leaves, green chillies and ginger-garlic paste.

Process in a mixer, remove into a bowl with a squeeze of lime and serve as an accompaniment to main dishes.

Sweet and Sour Chutney

Sweet and sour chutneys are often made as an accompaniment to most dishes.

Ingredients

> Tomatoes – 5
> Sugar – 1 teaspoon
> Dry red chilli – 1
> Ginger-garlic paste – ½ teaspoon
> Paanch phoron (five-spice blend) – ¼ teaspoon
> Slivers of ginger – ¼ teaspoon
> Oil – 1½ teaspoons
> Salt to taste

Method

Heat oil in a vessel, add dry red chilli, paanch phoron and ginger-garlic paste. Temper and stir, then add finely chopped tomatoes, along with slivers of ginger, sugar and salt. Cook chutney on a low flame for fifteen minutes till done.

Variation: Chutneys are also made with raw mango or dates or tamarind juice or grated coconut, or a mix-and-match of various ingredients.

Chicken and Meat Recipes

Hameen

Ingredients

- Chicken – 500 grams (one small whole chicken)
- Chicken livers – ¼ cup
- Rice – ¼ cup
- Oil – 1 tablespoon
- Onions – 2
- Garlic cloves – 3
- Cinammon stick – 1 inch
- Cinammon powder – ½ teaspoon
- Cloves – 3
- Cardamom pods – 3
- Bay leaf – 1
- Garam masala – 2 teaspoons
- Tomato pulp – 2 tablespoons
- Almonds – 6
- Raisins – 6
- Tamarind pulp – 1 teaspoon
- Salt to taste
- Water for cooking

Method

Take a small whole chicken, wash, rub with salt and keep aside. In a shallow pan, heat 1 tablespoon oil and brown chicken on both sides on a low flame for five minutes. Remove from stove and keep aside.

Soak rice in a bowl, mix half the quantity of rice with salt, garam masala, chopped almonds and raisins, and cook till soft. In a small pan, cook chicken livers separately in ¼ cup water till tender and mix with rice. Stuff this mixture into the open cavity of the whole chicken, sew with twine and keep aside.

Heat oil in a casserole, brown sliced onions on a low flame, temper with bay leaf, cinnamon stick, cloves, cardamom pods, garam masala and cinnamon powder. Add the remaining rice with salt, tomato pulp, tamarind pulp, finely chopped coriander leaves and mint leaves, cook till soft and tender.

Simultaneously, preheat an oven at 250 degrees Celsius and bake chicken in the oven for 1 ½ hours at the same temperature, till golden brown. Remove from oven and place in the casserole of rice. Add 1 cup water, cover with lid and simmer on a low flame for five minutes, till the rice and roast chicken are soaked in a light gravy. Serve in a large serving platter for Shabbath dinner. The leftovers are kept in the refrigerator for Saturday lunch.

Chicken Chittani

Ingredients

> Chicken – 500 grams
> Oil – 2 tablespoons
> Onions – 2
> Tomatoes – 2
> Red chillies – 2
> Ginger-garlic paste – 1 tablespoon
> Coriander powder – 2 teaspoons
> Cumin powder – 2 teaspoons

Tamarind pulp – 1 tablespoon

Sugar – ½ teaspoon

Salt to taste

Water as per requirement

Method

Soak chicken pieces in water, wash and keep aside.

Heat oil in a casserole, add chopped onions and sauté till brown. Add ginger-garlic paste and whole red chillies. Sauté for two minutes, then add powdered cumin and coriander, stir, and add finely chopped tomatoes. Cook till tomatoes are soft, then add tamarind pulp, sugar, salt with 1 cup water. Add chicken pieces, cook on a medium flame, cover, cook on a low flame for thirty to thirty-five minutes till chicken is tender and gravy thickens. Serve hot with rice.

Arook

Ingredients

Minced meat – 500 grams

Spring onions – 2

Turmeric – ½ teaspoon

Red chilli powder – ½ teaspoon

Small green chilli – 1

Black pepper powder – ½ teaspoon

Refined flour – 2 tablespoons

Eggs – 2 beaten

Oil for frying

Salt to taste

Method

Pressure-cook mince meat, then drain stock. Place the meat in a pan and cook on a low flame till dry. Cool and place in a bowl. Add turmeric, red chilli powder, finely chopped green chilli, finely chopped spring onions. Add flour and salt and mix well. Crack eggs and add and mix well. Cover and refrigerate for one hour, then shape into small balls with greased palms. Heat oil in a kadhai, drop mince balls into it and deep fry till golden brown. Remove with a slotted spoon, drain oil and serve hot as a snack or with a combination of dal and rice.

Variation: Minced mutton or mashed fish can be used to make these fritters.

Mahasha

Ingredients

Vegetables
Bell peppers – 2
Tomatoes – 2
Aubergines – 2

Filling
Chicken mince – 500 grams
Basmati rice – 1 cup
Oil – 2 tablespoons
Onion – 1
Ginger-garlic paste – 1 tablespoon
Cinnamon powder – 1 ½ teaspoons
Turmeric – 1 teaspoon
Fresh lemon juice – 1 teaspoon
Sugar – 1 teaspoon

Tamarind paste – 1 ½ teaspoons

Fresh mint leaves – ¼ cup

Fresh coriander leaves – 1 cup

Salt to taste

Water for cooking

Method

Cut a circle around the stems of vegetables, remove the top and keep aside to use as caps to cover them later. Scoop the seeds out of the capsicums, tomatoes and aubergines with a teaspoon.

For the filling, soak rice in a bowl of water, wash and boil in a vessel till cooked and tender. Boil the mince, drain excess water, place in a pan with ½ teaspoon oil and simmer on a low flame till dry. Put mince in a bowl and mix with rice, salt, turmeric powder, ginger-garlic paste, cinnamon powder, sugar, tamarind paste, finely chopped mint and coriander leaves. Stir and cool.

This filling is stuffed in the hollow of each vegetable and sealed with their caps.

Next, preheat an oven at 180 degrees Celsius. Grease a shallow baking dish, fill with 1 cup water, arrange the stuffed vegetables on the baking tray, bake for 15 minutes till cooked and serve hot.

Variation: you can also use cucumbers, zucchini and onion.

Fish Recipes

Fish Curry

Ingredients

Fish slices – 500 grams

Turmeric – ½ teaspoon

Nigella seeds or kalonji – ¼ teaspoon
Dry red chilli – 1
Bay leaf – 1
Onion – 1 large
Red chilli powder – 1 teaspoon
Coriander powder – ¼ teaspoon
Cumin powder – ¼ teaspoon
Water – 1 cup
Salt for marinating and curry
Oil for frying fish

Method

Wash fish pieces, marinate in salt and turmeric, then wash again and pat dry. Heat oil is heated in a kadhai, fry the fish pieces till they are golden brown, remove from the kadhai with a slotted spoon and keep aside.

In the same kadhai, temper nigella seeds or kalonji, whole dry red chillies and a bay leaf. Add chopped onions and brown. Next, add a bowl of water along with salt, turmeric, powdered chilli, coriander and cumin. The fish slices are added last, then the curry is cooked on a medium flame till the gravy thickens. It is served hot with rice.

Egg and Vegetarian Recipes

Mahmoosa

Ingredients

Eggs – 6
Onion – 2

Potatoes – 2 large

Oil – ¾ cup

Salt to taste

This simple recipe is made with sliced onions, potatoes and eggs. Oil is heated in a pan, in which the sliced onions are fried and sprinkled with salt. A layer of fried onions are spread on the base of the same pan, and fried potatoes are layered over them. This is cooked on a low flame. In another bowl, eggs are broken and dropped, one after another, on top of the layers of onions and potatoes. The pan is covered with a lid and cooked for a few minutes, till the eggs are done.

Cheese Sambouseks

Ingredients

Dough

Refined flour – 2 cups

Oil – ¼ cup

Sugar 3/4 teaspoon

Salt – ¼ teaspoon

Filling

Cheddar cheese – 400 grams

Eggs – 2

Method

In a large bowl, mix flour, salt, sugar and oil. Add water and knead into a dough, cover and keep aside.

In another bowl, make a filling with grated cheese and whisked eggs.

Divide dough into lemon-sized balls, place on a board, roll into ¼ inch puris with a rolling pin. Place a teaspoon of filling in the centre of each puri, shape like a crescent, seal and crimp. Arrange sambouseks on a greased baking tray, bake in a preheated oven at 180 degrees Celsius for fifteen minutes till they puff up and are done.

Cucumber Zalata

Ingredients

> Cucumbers – 3
> Green chillies – 1 teaspoon
> Ginger – 2 teaspoons
> Garlic – 2 teaspoons
> Mint – 2 tablespoons
> Vinegar – 3/4 cup
> Sugar – 1 tablespoon
> Salt to taste

Method

Peel cucumbers, scoop out seeds, cut into 1 ½ inch thin slices, add salt and marinate for an hour. Drain excess water.

In another bowl, combine chopped chillies, ginger, garlic and mint leaves with sugar. Add cucumber slices, mix and keep aside. Boil vinegar in a small vessel on a low flame, add to cucumber mixture, cool and store in glass bottle. Serve as an accompaniment to main dishes.

Soups

Chicken Soup

This soup is known as marag or murug soup. It is supposed to cure colds and other ailments and is made during winter months.

Ingredients

    Chicken pieces – 300 grams
    Garlic – 1 clove
    Pumpkin – 150 grams
    Bottle gourd or lauki – 150 grams
    Carrots – 4
    Green beans – 150 grams
    Lemon – 1
    Coriander leaves – 1 tablespoon
    Water – 5 glasses
    Salt to taste

Method

Wash chicken pieces. Peel, wash and cube vegetables and keep in a bowl of water. Boil water in a large vessel and add chicken pieces with salt, crushed garlic, pumpkin, bottle gourd, tomatoes, carrots, stringed beans, lemon juice and coriander leaves. Cook for thirty-five to forty minutes, till vegetables are soft and chicken is tender. Serve hot in soup bowls.

Optional: You can add dumplings when the chicken is almost done.

Variation: The same recipe can be made with fish cuts. Debone the fish before adding it to the soup. It is known as ekjosh.

Sweet and Sour Chicken Soup

This soup is also known as khatta soup.

Ingredients

Chicken – 300 grams
Beetroot – ½ cup
Lemon juice – 2 tablespoons
Water – 5 glasses
Salt to taste

Method

Boil chicken pieces in water. Add cubed beetroot, lemon juice and salt. Cook for thirty-five minutes until the chicken is done. Serve hot in soup bowls.

Kooba Dumplings

Ingredients

Minced chicken – 300 grams
Oil – 2 tablespoons
Ginger-garlic paste – 1 tablespoon
Rice flour – ¼ cup
Semolina – ¼ cup
Black pepper powder – ¼ teaspoon
Coriander leaves – 1 tablespoon
Salt to taste
Water

Method

In a bowl, place minced chicken, add 1 teaspoon oil, salt, finely chopped onion, ginger-garlic paste, black pepper powder and a few coriander leaves and mix. With greased palms, roll this mixture into lemon-sized balls.

In another bowl, make a covering for the dumplings. Mix rice flour, semolina, salt, add a little water and knead into a dough. Divide the dough into slightly larger balls than the chicken and, with moist palms, flatten balls into small puris. Place one minced chicken ball in the centre of a puri, cover from all sides and shape into a dumpling. Do the same with the rest of the puris and chicken balls. Poach these dumplings in stews or soups for twenty minutes. Serve hot in soup bowls.

Hilbeh

Ingredients

    Fenugreek seeds – 1 tablespoon

    Hot water – 1 cup

    Coriander leaves – 1 cup

    Garlic cloves – 3

    Green chilli – 1

    Ginger – 1 ½ inch

    Lemon juice – ¾ teaspoon

    Salt to taste

Method

Soak fenugreek seeds in a bowl of warm water. Cover and let stand for six to eight hours. Drain water, wash fenugreek seeds, process in a blender with 2 tablespoons of water and make a smooth paste.

Open the lid of blender, add salt, lemon juice, chopped coriander leaves, finely diced ginger-garlic-green chilli, process again and serve hilbe in a bowl.

Hilbe is served as an accompaniment to aloo makala and hameen.

Desserts

Baba

Ingredients

Dough

Plain flour – ¾ cup
Refined flour – ½ cup
Sugar – 1¼ tablespoons
Butter – 1½ tablespoons
Vegetable oil – ½ tablespoon
Vanilla essence – ¾ teaspoon
Egg – 1
Water – ¾ cup
Salt to taste

Filling

Vegetable oil – 1½ teaspoons
Seedless dates – 125 grams
Sesame seeds
Water

Method

In a bowl, mix flour, butter, oil, sugar, salt and vanilla essence. Knead into a dough with a little warm water, wrap the dough in a damp cloth and refrigerate for thirty minutes.

Meanwhile, in a heavy-bottomed pan, add oil, dates and water. Cover and simmer on a low flame for fifteen minutes till the dates soften. Mash into a pulp with a hand masher and cool.

To make the sweet-savoury babas, take out the dough from the refrigerator and divide into small balls. With greased palms, flatten the dough into circles; shape into 'cups', place some of the date filling in the centre of each cup, close it and seal the edges. Roll into a ball and flatten into ½ inch puris by hand and place on a platter.

Crack and whisk an egg in a small bowl and brush the babas with the egg wash. Sprinkle them with sesame seeds and arrange on a baking tray. Preheat oven at 200 degrees Celsius, place the tray in oven and bake the babas for fifteen minutes. Cool and store in a container.

Kaka Rings

Ingredients

Plain flour – ¾ cup
Refined flour – ½ cup
Sugar – 1 ¼ tablespoons sugar
Caraway seeds – ¼ teaspoon
Egg – 1
Butter – 1 ½ tablespoons
Water – ¾ cup
Vegetable oil – ½ tablespoon
Vanilla essence – ¾ teaspoon
Salt to taste

Method

In a bowl, mix flour, butter, oil, sugar, salt, caraway seeds and vanilla essence. Knead the mixture into a dough with warm water, wrap in a damp cloth and refrigerate for thirty minutes. After that, divide the dough into lemon-sized balls. On a board, shape each ball into a thin strand and then shape into 1½ inch circular rings, like bracelets. Seal the edges and arrange on a baking tray.

In another small bowl, crack and whisk an egg and brush the kaka rings with the egg wash. Preheat an oven at 200 degrees Celsius. Place the rings in the oven and bake for fifteen minutes. Remove from oven, cool and store in a container.

Agar-Agar Jelly

According to the Jewish dietary law, agar-agar is the perfect dessert as it can be served with both vegetarian and non-vegetarian dishes.

Ingredients

Agar-agar or China-grass powder – 2 tablespoons
Sugar – 5 to 6 teaspoons
Water – 4 ½ cups

Method

Soak agar-agar powder in a pan of water and drain excess water. Dissolve the mixture in 4 ½ cups of water, add sugar and cook on a low flame. Stir till the liquid thickens. Remove from flame, pour into a jelly mould, cool at room temperature for half an hour till it sets, refrigerate and serve as dessert.

Optional: When the agar-agar mixture starts thickening on the stove, add a few drops of vanilla or one teaspoon of rose sherbet or both, for flavour and colour.

Agar-agar jelly can also be made with milk, instead of water, using this recipe, which is served with vegetarian meals.

6

The Bene Ephraim Jews of Andhra Pradesh

I decided to start my study of Indian Jewish cuisine with the Bene Ephraim Jews, as I was fascinated by the image of the small Bene Ephraim synagogue at Machilipatnam near Vijayawada in Andhra Pradesh. Bene Ephraim in Hebrew means 'children of Ephraim'.

I had the email address of Mukthipudi Jaya Kumar Jacob, fondly known as Jaya Kumar, whose family looks after the synagogue at Machilipatnam. He is an associate professor of environmental studies at Chirala Engineering College, Andhra Pradesh. Once I established contact with him, I embarked on my journey.

It was an unusual experience, quite in contrast to my urban Jewish experiences in Maharasthra, Kerala and West Bengal. Machilipatnam gave me a rare insight into another world. Here,

some members of the Bene Ephraim community still live in
rural areas.

A Rural Jewish Household

The Vijayawada International Airport at Gannavaram,
Vijayawada, is small, neat and clean, decorated with copies of
kalamkari fabric designs, leather puppets and Kondapalli toys made
of wood, which depict village life in Andhra Pradesh. Jaya Kumar
received me. He had hired a taxi to Machilipatnam for us.

It was mid-monsoon and the air was humid, but the drive to
Machilipatnam unfolded a refreshing landscape. The taxi drove past

villages which had huts with thatched roofs made of palm leaves. I could also smell the fragrance of sea air. The taxi sped past fields with farmers tilling the land, and ponds, lakes, orchards and banana groves, lined with tall trees of palm, coconut, teak and drumstick.

The taxi veered past herds of buffaloes, cows, goats, sheep and even flocks of country chickens running around on the dust roads. All along the drive, there were roadside stalls selling cold drinks, coffee, tea, snacks, chopped areca nut or supari, basic groceries, mounds of tender coconut and kalamkari handkerchiefs.

At Machilipatnam, I saw temples painted in bright colours, churches and mosques, and the city square, which had a fountain with four mermaids. Almost all the houses had on display a protective mask of Pothuraju, with a long, curved moustache and red horns. When the taxi turned towards my hotel, I saw a huge statue of the saintly spiritual master Sai Baba of Shirdi, which was sculpted with a halo of Shesh Nag, the seven-hooded serpent of Lord Vishnu.

After checking into the hotel, I rushed to the Bene Ephraim Community Synagogue as the Jewish community had already collected there to meet me and to attend Shabbath prayers. Some had travelled long distances to reach Machilipatnam, as they were from other cities, towns and villages of Andhra Pradesh.

The synagogue was in the suburbs, surrounded by bungalows where the Jacob family and their relatives lived, although some of their family members also live in Israel. It was small and built in a walled courtyard, painted in different shades of blue, with the Star of David and a menorah. There was a narrow veranda, a corridor with small windows, an extra doorway facing the horizon and a mezuzah at the doorpost of the synagogue. The heikal or the ark was at the far end of the synagogue, facing west, where a torah was kept in a cabinet, covered with a silk curtain. The centre of the synagogue had a small wooden railing, behind which there was the bima or teva, a slightly raised platform from where the hazzan leads the prayers.

This is a small synagogue, so women and young girls were seated on chairs in the last row, while men and boys sat in the front row. In larger synagogues, according to custom, Jewish men sit on the left and women on the right. I was introduced to Jaya Kumar's brother Dan, the hazzan of the synagogue, his family and other members of the Bene Ephraim Jewish community. According to Jewish custom, the men were wearing kippas while the women had covered their heads with scarves or the ends of their saris. The Tallit, a prayer shawl, is also worn by Jewish men for Yom Kippur prayers, religious events and some rituals.

Andhra Pradesh also has a synagogue in Chebrolu near Guntur.

In Machilipatnam, I discovered that the Bene Ephraim Jews had a deep faith in Jewish life and a desire to preserve their heritage.

It was a pleasant evening and the pink shades of the sky were darkening, Dan stood on the teva chanting Shabbath prayers while the congregation followed him. Soon after, two young girls sang Hebrew songs accompanied by Jaya Kumar on the violin. After this, he gave a solo performance playing Hebrew prayer tunes, which ended with applause. I was introduced to the congregation as Jaya Kumar distributed the questionnaire that I had formulated to learn about Jewish cuisine.

That night, I had Shabbath dinner at Dan's home with his entire family. His home was next to the synagogue. The family had prepared fried bhindi, potato curry, fried fish, fish-egg curry, parathas, rice and a variety of spicy chutneys made with gongura leaf, tomato, tamarind, sesame and crushed peanut, along with a bottle of gongura leaf pickle, which had pride of place on the table. Gongura leaves, also known as sorrel leaves, are blanched in boiling water and drained to reduce their sour taste before they are added to vegetables, chicken curry and other dishes, or before being made into chutney.

Gongura Leaves and Accompaniments

The next day, I went to the Manginapudi seashore in an autorickshaw. These autos carry four to six people, all crammed in with each other. Sometimes some passengers sit next to the driver. The sea had a gateway of sculpted dolphins next to a Hanuman temple, a cart of seashells and vendors of tender-coconut water. Two fishermen were returning with a catch of fish, placed in a box and carried on an oar. One of them was wearing a tight loincloth and the other was wearing a mundu or a sarong tied around his waist. They stood covered with fine sand, surrounded by a group of women buying freshly caught fish. I noticed that the women were wearing saris and had flowers in their hair. The Jewish women of the Bene Ephraim Jewish community wear the same attire. Jewish men wear shirts over trousers but prefer to wear a mundu or sarong at home.

We stopped at the vegetable market, which was a built space, where vendors were selling vegetables and fruit. The market walls were painted in red ochre, decorated with kolam patterns, best described as curlicues. It is a ritualistic art form. Traditionally, these are painted by hand, with rice-flour paste or white powder, at the entrance of most south Indian homes. The market was tidy, and there was a variety of vegetables and fruits, like banana clusters on long stalks, potatoes, onions, bhindi, cabbage, cauliflower, pumpkin, bottle gourd, spinach, gongura leaves, curry leaves, coriander leaves, fresh mint, tamarind blossoms, raw mangoes, ripe mangoes, berries and fiery hot Guntur chillies.

At the entrance of the market, a woman was selling kalamkari napkins, which are multipurpose, as they can be used to wipe perspiration, keep paan leaves damp or cover food. In a lane nearby, women were making kalamkari designs with block-printing techniques on fabric.

I then visited a Jewish home near the synagogue. At the doorway I saw a kolam with the design of a star, which was painted a little off centre, so that one does not step on it. The lady of the house, whom I had met the day before at the synagogue, invited me in. I noticed that the interior was urban, with religious artifacts from Israel, along with framed family photographs on the walls. The kitchen had steel utensils, plasticware, a filter-coffee container and a stone mortar and pestle to grind masala. I learned that nowadays they prefer electric mixers to make chutneys or batter for idli, vada and dosa. The fridge had a vessel filled to the brim with medu-vada batter, made of fermented rice and lentils, for the next day's breakfast. And, for dinner, she had planned to make sambhar with toor dal or pigeon-peas, along with rice and vegetables. It was midday, so the lady invited me to join the family for lunch. The table was laid with drumstick curry, potatoes, brinjals cooked in tamarind sauce, dal and rice, which was served with a helping of ghee, mango pickle, sesame chutney, boiled eggs and yogurt.

After lunch, she took me around her garden, which had gongura bushes, a luxuriant plant of curry leaves, pomegranate, guava, banana, grapevines and a drumstick tree. I was told that gongura leaves are essential in Telugu cuisine and that sometimes sun-dried fish and meat are also added to some vegetable curries.

That evening, I visited an old cemetery situated next to a French monument, where I saw Dutch, French and British graves, along with graves of the Christian community and the Bene Ephraim Jews of Machilipatnam.

The Bene Ephraim Jews follow the dietary law and keep their kitchen kosher, with separate utensils and dishes for dairy and meat. And if, by mistake, meat is cooked in a vessel used for milk, the vessel is washed with warm water and not used for twenty-four hours. The Bene Ephraim Jews maintain four to five hours of difference between having milk and meat dishes.

Leafy vegetables are soaked in salt water and checked for worms, as they don't eat insects, considered to be non-kosher. Meat or chicken or fish are soaked in salt water and washed properly before they are cooked. During festivals, food is made in vessels that have been washed in warm water. Earlier, Telugu Jews used to serve food on plantain or lotus leaves, but now they use steel thalis, melamine plates or disposable plates.

In the absence of a shohet, an elder of the Bene Ephraim community prepares kosher meat in accordance with the Jewish dietary law.

Fish curry and rice is the staple diet of the Bene Ephraim Jews. During summer months, they also make boiled eggs or a simple one-dish meal of lemon rice or curd rice or tamarind rice or vegetarian biryani or egg pulao, which is served with a variety of chutneys, pickles and poppadums.

In winter, spicy fried rice is made with chicken curry or fried chicken or potato curry, while vegetables are cooked with dried fish or dried meat along with boiled eggs as an accompaniment. The Bene Ephraim Jews have a preference for spinach, which is served with a dal-rice or sambhar-rice or rasam-rice combination.

Rice dishes, like lemon rice or tamarind rice, are made with plain white masuri rice or parboiled rice. Sambhar is made with toor dal, while rasam, which is also known as tamarind soup, is made with dal water. When meat or fish dishes are not cooked, the Bene Ephraim Jews make curd rice or vegetable curry with rice and eat it along with a bowl of yogurt, which is served separately.

Payasam or rice pudding is made as a dessert, with rice, milk and sugar, garnished with cardamom powder. A similar recipe is made with vermicelli. As milk is used in these recipes, both payasam and vermicelli are only served with vegetarian dishes (recipe on page 141).

When rice pudding is served with meat dishes, it is made with rice cooked in coconut milk and jaggery, and garnished with cardamom powder and broken nuts.

FESTIVALS AND OCCASIONS

Shabbath

The Bene Ephraim Jews say their prayers in Hebrew or read them out from books where the pronunciations of Hebrew words are transliterated and written in Telugu.

For Shabbath prayers, they buy bread or buns from a bakery or make wheat-flour chapattis. Two candles are lit by the woman of the house, prayers are said over bread and a glass of grape juice and the Shabbath meal is served. In the absence of kosher wine, homemade grape juice is used as a substitute. I was told by the women of the Bene Ephraim Jewish community that the Shabbath meal is made according to the season, so that it does not spoil till the next day. Of course, with refrigerators, now any type of food can be made, but some foods are still cooked according to season, as per tradition.

Rosh Hashanah

The Bene Ephraim Jews begin the Jewish New Year with apples dipped in honey. They also have dates, pomegranates, seasonal fruits, sweet biscuits and savoury vadas.

They donate clothes to needy community members and give gifts to each other during the New Year.

Yom Kippur

The Bene Ephraim Jews fast on Yom Kippur. This fast is broken with grape juice, sweetened lemon juice, soft drinks, cakes and fruit, followed by a simple meal of dal rice or curd rice and sweets.

Simchat Torah

This festival marks the completion of reading the Torah. It is celebrated with chicken curry, fried rice or pulao and savoury medu vada. Payasam is eaten for dessert.

If vegetarian dishes are made for Simchat Torah, vermicelli is cooked with milk and jaggery.

Purim

During Purim, different types of cakes are made, along with savoury fritters or lentil vadas or murukku.

Hanukkah

To celebrate Hanukkah, candles are lit, and sweet laddoos known as ariselu are made with powdered rice and jaggery (recipe on pages 140–141)..

Passover

A traditional Passover table or Seder is set with a ritualistic meal. It is held by the Bene Ephraim Jewish community of Andhra Pradesh in the courtyard of their synagogue. Often, there is one main table for the hazzan who leads the prayers and other tables for the congregation. Candles are lit on each table, next to the Passover platter, which hold handmade matzo bread or chapatti made with unleavened wheat-flour dough. The Passover platter also holds dates, bowls of salt water, radish paste, bitter leaves, boiled eggs, apples and the roasted neck bone of a chicken.

Nowadays, the Bene Ephraim Jews receive matzo packets from Israel for Passover prayers, yet they prepare their own matzo chapattis for the Passover Seder. Matzo received from Israel is often distributed at the synagogue to those present for Passover prayers.

Biryani is made with meat for Passover dinner, which is served with chicken curry, potato curry and gongura leaf chutney.

RECIPES

Curry

Ingredients

> Meat/Chicken/Fish – 500 grams
> Onions – 2
> Oil – ½ cup
> Mustard seeds – ¼ teaspoon
> Curry leaves – 7
> Ginger-garlic paste – 1 tablespoon
> Green chillies – 2
> Red chilli powder – 1 teaspoon

Turmeric powder – ½ teaspoon

Cumin powder – 1 teaspoon

Water – 8 glasses

Coriander leaves – 2 tablespoons

Method

Heat oil in a heavy vessel and temper mustard seeds. Add sliced onions and fry with curry leaves, ginger-garlic paste, chopped green chillies, red chilli powder, turmeric, cumin and salt. Then add water and cook for ten minutes on a low flame. Then add meat or chicken or fish pieces to the curry, mix well, and cook on a medium flame or pressure-cook for twenty-five whistles. The finished curry is garnished with chopped coriander leaves and served with rice.

Variation: Two chopped tomatoes are added to lend flavour to the curry. One cup coconut milk can also be added to thicken the curry. One tablespoon tamarind extract is often added to fish curries.

Note: If meat is added to the curry, pressure cook for thirty-five minutes and if fish is added to the curry, cook in a pan for seven minutes.

Optional: Boiled eggs are served as an accompaniment to most curry-based meals.

Tamarind extract is often added to fish curries.

Fish Recipes

The Bene Ephraim Jews have freshwater fish or fish caught from the sea. According to the dietary law, they have fish with scales.

Fried Fish Heads

This dish is specially made for Rosh Hashanah. See recipe on page 32.

It is served with a vegetable curry or sambhar or chicken curry or rice and banana chips.

Fish Eggs

Delicate and succulent fish eggs are made on festive occasions for special guests.

Ingredients

Fish eggs – 500 grams
Turmeric powder – 1 teaspoon
Cumin powder – 1½ teaspoon
Red chilli powder – 2 teaspoons
Oil for frying – ½ cup
Salt to taste

Method

Wash fish eggs, sprinkle with turmeric and salt, cook in steam or in a pressure cooker on a low flame, till done. When cooled, place these delicate fish eggs on a platter, cut carefully into pieces so that they do not crumble and keep aside. Heat oil in an open-mouthed vessel, and add fish eggs, along with red chilli powder, turmeric, cumin and salt. Let the fish eggs cook in their own juices on a low flame for five minutes. Remove and serve with rice, along with fish curry and vegetables.

Chicken Recipes

Chicken Curry with Gongura or Sorrel Leaves

Ingredients

Chicken – 500 grams
Gongura leaves – 1 cup
Oil – 3 tablespoons

Poppy seeds – 1 teaspoon

Grated coconut – 1 teaspoon

Mustard seeds – ¼ teaspoon

Cumin seeds – ½ teaspoon

Dry red chillies – 2

Onions – 3

Green chillies – 2

Curry leaves – 10

Garlic cloves – 2

Ginger-garlic paste – 1 tablespoon

Red chilli powder – 1 teaspoon

Turmeric powder – 1 teaspoon

Cumin powder – 1 teaspoon

Coriander powder – 1 teaspoon

Cinnamon – 1 medium stick

Cloves – 2

Cardamom pods – 2

Garam masala – 1 teaspoon

Tomato puree – 1 ½ tablespoon

Sugar – ½ teaspoon

Water

Salt to taste

Method

Wash chicken pieces and marinate in ginger-garlic paste, powdered red chilli, turmeric, cumin, coriander and salt for fifteen minutes and keep aside.

Cut gongura leaf stems, wash, chop, place in a vessel, add 1 glass of water and boil on a high flame. Cook leaves till they wilt, remove from stove, cool on a platter, drain to remove the rather tart taste of gongura leaves. Roughly mash the leaves with a crusher and keep aside.

Process the poppy seeds and grated coconut with a tablespoon of water, make a paste and keep aside in a bowl.

Heat oil in a deep vessel, temper mustard seeds, curry leaves, dry red chillies, diced green chillies, cinnamon stick, cloves and cardamom. Add sliced onions and fry till transparent. Add chicken pieces, turmeric, salt, ginger-garlic paste, powdered red chilli, cumin, coriander, garam masala, poppy seed and coconut paste, tomato puree with ½ teaspoon sugar and mix well. Add 2 glasses of water, cover with a lid and cook on a medium flame for twenty-five minutes.

Reduce the flame, remove lid and add boiled gongura leaves to the chicken curry. Stir and cook on a low flame for ten minutes till chicken is tender. Remove from stove and serve with rice.

Variation: Mutton can be made with this recipe and cooked for thirty-five minutes.

Note: Chicken curry with gongura or sorrel leaves has a rather tart flavour.

Rice Recipes

Festive Rice with Spices

Ingredients

    Oil – 1 tablespoon
    Red rice – 2 cups
    Onions – 1
    Tomatoes – 2
    Garlic cloves – 2

Green chillies – 2
Cloves – 2
Cardamom pods – 2
Cinnamon – 1 medium stick
Turmeric powder – ¼ teaspoon
Red chilli powder – 1 teaspoon
Cumin powder – ½ teaspoon
Coriander powder – ½ teaspoon
Coriander leaves – 1 tablespoon
Water for soaking rice

Method

Soak red rice in a bowl of warm water for twenty minutes, wash, drain and keep aside. In a deep vessel, boil water and add salt, powdered turmeric, red chilli powder, powdered cumin-coriander and rice. Cook on a medium flame till rice is almost tender and cover with lid.

Simultaneously, heat oil in a small pan, temper finely chopped garlic, curry leaves, diced green chillies and sliced onions and fry till the onions are browned. Add cloves, cinnamon, cardamom pods, finely chopped tomatoes, stir and sauté. Mix this masala with the rice prepared earlier, cook on a low flame for fifteen minutes till rice softens, garnish with coriander leaves, remove from stove and serve hot with chicken curry.

Variation: You can add a few drops of different edible colours to cook white rice.

Note: This recipe is made during festivals as it lends colour and flavour to the festive dinner.

Tamarind Rice

Ingredients

> Rice – 1 cup
> Turmeric – ½ teaspoon
> Tamarind juice – ¼ cup
> Mustard seeds – ½ teaspoon
> Curry leaves – 7
> Green chilli – 1 large
> Peanuts – ¼ cup
> Oil – ¼ cup
> Water – 3 cups
> Salt to taste

Method

Boil water in a vessel and add rice with salt and turmeric. When rice is cooked, mix tamarind juice and cook for a few more minutes till the water evaporates. In another pan, heat oil and temper mustard seeds along with curry leaves, chopped green chillies and peanuts. Add to the tamarind rice. This one-dish meal is made for Shabbath and other Jewish festivals.

Curd Rice or Yogurt Rice

This is the perfect antidote to improve digestion and cool the system during summer months. Indian Jews have curd rice with vegetarian meals.

Ingredients

> Cooked rice – 1 cup
> Yogurt – 1 ½ cups

Oil – 1 tablespoon
Mustard seeds – 1 teaspoon
Curry leaves – 5-6
Dry red chillies – 2
Diced green chillies – 2
Chopped coriander leaves – 1 teaspoon

Method

In a vessel, mix cooked rice with salt and yogurt. Heat oil in a pan and temper mustard seeds with curry leaves, dry red chillies and diced green chillies. Mix these with the rice-yogurt mixture. Garnish with chopped coriander leaves.

Biryani

This is a bit different from the Bene Israeli biryani recipe given earlier.

Ingredients

Basmati or any long-grained rice – 2 cups
Meat pieces – 500 grams
Ginger-garlic paste – 1 tablespoon
Garam masala – 1 tablespoon
Chopped coriander leaves – 1 ½ tablespoons
Green chillis – 2
Turmeric powder – ¼ teaspoon
Red chilli powder – 1 teaspoon
Cumin powder – 1 teaspoon
Peppercorn – 8
Cinnamon stick – 2 inches
Cardamom pods – 3

Cumin seeds – ¼ teaspoon

Onions – 2

Saffron – few strands

Garam masala for garnishing – ¼ teaspoon

Oil – ½ cup

Water – 8 glasses

Salt to taste

Method

Soak Basmati rice or any long-grained rice in a bowl of water and keep aside. Wash medium-sized meat pieces, marinate in ginger-garlic paste and garam masala with chopped coriander leaves, crushed green chilli, turmeric powder, red chilli powder, cumin, salt and a squeeze of lime. Pressure-cook the meat for fifteen minutes with peppercorns, cinnamon, cloves and cardamoms and keep aside. Brown onions with finely chopped green chillies in a heavy vessel with hot oil. Take a small amount of the meat stock, add to this and sauté, add water and cook for twenty-five minutes. In another vessel, cook rice with salt till almost done, drain and keep aside. Place one portion of the rice in a platter and mix with saffron, which has been dissolved in warm water prior to being added. Saffron lends a pleasant colour and flavour to the biryani. Cook the biryani on a low flame and pour the remaining meat stock over it. Arrange layers of white rice and saffron above the cooked meat and garnish with crisp fried onions and sprinkle with powdered garam masala along with any remaining saffron water. Cover the vessel with a lid, seal with dough and cook on a low flame till the aroma of biryani fills the house. The biryani is served hot.

Variation: Biryani can also be made with vegetables like peas, potatoes, carrots and fresh beans.

Vegetarian Recipes

Stir-fried Spinach

Ingredients

- Spinach leaves – 250 grams
- Water – 1 cup
- Onion – 1 large
- Garlic – 4 cloves
- Green chillies – 2
- Tomatoes – 2
- Oil – 2 tablespoons

Method

Wash spinach leaves, chop, blanch in water, drain and keep aside. Heat oil in a vessel and fry sliced onions with diced garlic, slit green chillies, chopped tomatoes and salt. Add spinach leaves, cook for a few minutes and serve with a combination of dal-rice or meat dishes.

Pachadi

Ingredients

- Yogurt – 400 grams
- Oil – 1 tablespoon
- Mustard seeds – ¼ teaspoon
- Curry leaves – 7
- Dry red chillies – 2
- Green chilli – 1 large
- Coriander leaves – 1 tablespoon
- Salt to taste

Method

Mix yogurt with salt to taste and keep aside. Heat oil in a small pan and temper mustard seeds with curry leaves, dry red chillies and diced green chillies. Mix with the yogurt and garnish with chopped coriander leaves. This is the same recipe used for curd rice.

Variation: You can add vegetables such as spinach, which is washed, chopped and blanched, or fruit such as cubed pineapple or ripe mango, which are added to a bowl of yogurt.

Chutneys

A variety of chutneys are made by the Bene Ephraim Jews, such as gongura or sorrel leaf chutney, tomato chutney, raw mango chutney and sesame seed chutney. These are made as accompaniments to most dishes.

Sesame Seed Chutney

Ingredients

> Sesame seeds – ½ cup
> Dry red chillies – 3
> Turmeric – ¼ teaspoon
> Tamarind pulp – 2 teaspoons
> Mustard seeds – 1 teaspoon
> Curry leaves – 4
> Oil – 1 teaspoon
> Salt

Method

In a kadhai, roast sesame seeds with broken dry red chillies and ½ teaspoon sesame oil on a low flame for two minutes, stirring continuously. Remove from stove and cool; add turmeric, tamarind pulp and salt. Process this mixture into a thick chutney. Place in a serving bowl.

Heat ½ teaspoon sesame oil in a small pan and temper with mustard seeds and curry leaves. Add to sesame chutney, mix well and serve as an accompaniment to a variety of dishes.

Variation: Tomato and raw mango can also be used to make this chutney.

Gongura Leaf Chutney

Ingredients

> Gongura leaves – 250 grams
>
> Water – 1 cup
>
> Red chilli powder – 2 teaspoon
>
> Turmeric – ½ teaspoon
>
> Garlic – 6 cloves
>
> Coriander leaves – 1 tablespoon
>
> Curry leaves – 7
>
> Dry red chillies – 2
>
> Mustard seeds – ¼ teaspoon
>
> Salt to taste

Method

Wash gongura leaves, blanch in salt water, drain and grind on a stone mortar with a pestle or process in a mixer. Remove into a bowl. Add red chilli powder, turmeric, salt, crushed garlic and coriander leaves. In a small pan, heat oil and temper mustard seeds, curry leaves, dry red chillies and chopped garlic and add to the chutney. Serve as an accompaniment to main dishes.

Desserts

Sweet Laddoos or Sunnudalu

Ingredients

Urad dal or split skinless black gram – 1 cup
Jaggery – ¾ cup
Cardamom powder – 1 teaspoon
Ghee – ¼ cup

Method

In a bowl of water, soak urad dal for twenty minutes, wash, drain and spread on a clean cloth. Dry-roast urad dal in a griddle on a low flame, remove from stove, cool and process in a blender till powdered. Remove onto a platter, add cardamom-seed powder, grated jaggery, melted ghee and mix together. Grease palms, shape mixture into lemon-sized laddoos and store in a container.

Note: Bene Ephraim Jews break the fast of Yom Kippur with lemon juice, fruit juices and laddoos.

Ariselu Laddoos

Ingredients

New rice – 2 cups
Jaggery – 1 cup
Sesame seeds – ¼ cup
Oil for frying

Method

Roast rice, grind to a powder in a stone mortar with a pestle or process in a mixer. Mix powdered rice with melted jaggery, shape into laddoos and deep fry in oil. Remove with a slotted spoon, drain, place on a plate and sprinkle with sesame seeds.

Payasam

Ingredients

Rice – ½ cup
Sugar or jaggery – ¾ cup
Milk or coconut milk – 4 cups

Method

Soak rice in water for twenty minutes. Drain, mix with sugar or jaggery, then cook in milk till the rice is soft. It is served as a dessert with vegetarian dishes. If coconut milk is used instead of regular milk, it can be served with meat dishes.

Bobbatlu

Ingredients

Wheat-flour – 2 cups
Chana dal or moong dal – 1 cup
Jaggery – 1 cup
Ghee as needed
Water as needed

Method

Make a dough with wheat flour and water. Cut into balls, roll into a chapatti with a rolling pin and keep aside. Boil and mash chana dal or moong dal and mix with powdered jaggery. Place this mixture in the middle of a chapatti, seal its ends and roll again. Roasted on a griddle with ghee, till the chapatti puffs up. It is similar to the puran poli made by the Bene Israel Jews.

Rose Biscuits

These are also known as achu murukku. These rose biscuits are often made for the Jewish New Year and other festivals (recipe on page 90).

Grape Juice

Homemade grape juice is made with black grapes by Bene Ephraim Jews, which is used for Shabbath prayers and other Jewish festivals, like Passover. It is similar to the recipes made by the other Jews of India with the exception that salt, pepper and vinegar are added to the grapes (recipe on page 24).

A Bene Ephraim Jewish Lady Grates Coconut

7

The Bnei Menashe Jews
of Manipur

For years, I associated Manipur with its traditional dance form. The female dancers wear costumes of mirror-embellished dome-like skirts, velvet blouses, transparent veils held in place with conical head ornaments and garlands around the neck. They dance with slow, graceful movements. In contrast to the female dancers, the male drum dancers have energetic acrobatic body movements, similar to martial arts. The men wear dhotis with a colourful broadcloth around the waist and white turbans tied around their heads. The dancer playing Krishna wears a peacock-feather crown. Most themes of the Manipuri dance forms are centred on the theme of the Raslila of Lord Krishna and his beloved Radha, performed like a dance-drama. The epic Mahabharata mentions Manipur; when

Arjun had taken refuge there, he married the warrior princess, Chitrangada, who was accomplished in martial arts.

Imphal, the capital city of Manipur, has palaces, forts, temples, churches, mosques and a small synagogue. Interestingly, some buildings have pagoda-like structures similar to Japan. There are also urban housing societies and single- and double-storeyed houses with gabled roofs. Manipur is home to the Mapal Kangjeibung, one of the world's oldest polo grounds, which has statues of equestrian kings. The central marketplace is the hub of all activity.

Manipur's Bir Tikendrajit International Airport has a counter for artisanal chocolates made with raja chilli or king chilli. These are sold along with bars of roasted pumpkin-seed chocolates and boxes of cream-flavoured assorted chocolate cubes. Interestingly, the tea stall had chilli chai. Pumpkin seed and sunflower seed packets were also available, as they appeared to be popular with the people of Manipur.

Imphal has many different tribes, traditions and cultures. Its landscape has beautiful hills and valleys, and Manipur itself is known as the Land of Gold in the Meitei language, which is widely spoken there. The land is fertile, has water resources, rich flora and fauna, a generally pleasant climate, but cold winters. A river cuts through this city of lakes. Loktak Lake is a freshwater lake with abundant fish and is known for the Keibul Lamjao National Park, the only floating national park in the world, where herds of sangai deer, also known as brow-antlered deer, can be seen. It is the last natural refuge of this endangered species. The lake has floating swamp-like miniature-islands, which are created with catchments of aquatic vegetation.

The population of Manipur mainly consists of Hindus. According to an ancient tradition, some of their community dinners are cooked by Brahmins who are known for their culinary skills.

I came to know that there were Jews in Northeast India during the millenium. They are known as the Bnei Menashe Jews in Hebrew, which means 'children of Menashe' in English.

The Jewish population of this area continue to practice Judaism, as their ancestors did. Some of the Jews from Manipur have since emigrated to Israel. However, most of the Bnei Menashe Jews use their tribal name as a surname.

Most of the Jews of Northeast India speak different languages, depending on which state they live in. A small group lives in suburban Imphal, which is known as Langol Hebron Veng. This area is close to the regional boxing centre set up by Olympics champion Mary Kom. A large community of Jews lives in Churachandpur, a small town near Imphal. Here, the Shavei Israel Group of Northeast India looks after their emigration to Israel. The Jews of Manipur meet for Shabbath prayers at the Beith Shalom Synagogue.

A large number of the Bnei Menashe Jews have emigrated to Israel and the last few have plans to emigrate, so that they can be closer to their families.

Manipur Jews wear both Western wear and traditional attire. The women usually wear a woven wraparound sarong or mekhla, printed with intricate designs, with a blouse and shawl. Yet, like young people all over the world, the Bnei Menashe youth also wear trousers, jeans and T-shirts. A dhoti was traditionally worn by the men, but now they prefer Western clothes. Woollen shawls are worn by most people and often, women carry their babies on their back, tied with shawls. The shawls are woven in specific designs for men and women and also for different tribes.

In Imphal, the markets are housed in huge sprawling buildings, which also have places of worship, like a temple of Lord Krishna.

A large number of vendors are women, who one will find sitting in rows with their wares. In the food and crafts bazaar, orchids and exotic flowers of all colours are sold. Stacks of banana leaves cut into squares or rectangles, along with mounds of fruit, vegetables, roots, fiery hot raja chillis and bhut jolokia chillies are seen on sale. An entire area is allotted to vendors selling eggs and fish.

The market area is known as Ema Market, literally meaning Mother Market. It also has food stalls, where rice, dal or fish curry or fried snacks like pakodas are cooked in vessels placed over stoves. Hawkers sell fermented fish, dried strips of meat, soya soup in paper cups and pickled apple jam. The bazaar is also stacked with bamboo artifacts, knives and spears, and dolls dressed in the Manipuri dance attire. Women do brisk business, selling sweets made with puffed rice or sesame seeds cooked in jaggery, which are shaped like small pyramids, along with laddoos made with roasted, processed rice flour and sugar. Beside them are stalls of paan or betel leaf and areca nut or supari. Most Manipuris love paan, which is also widely available in roadside stalls.

A textile market nearby is also managed entirely by women.

It is a well-known fact that while the people of Manipur have retained their original lifestyle, they have evolved with time. They are known for their love of good food and no meal is complete without fish, which comes from Loktak Lake or fish farms and fish farming cooperatives of Manipur. Fish or chicken or meat are an essential part of most meals. They also make puris, potato curry, steamed rice and vegetable stew. They have a distinctive cuisine, which is often flavoured with fermented or sundried fish or dry meat. They also cook leafy vegetables in gravy, like mustard leaves, which are served with rice. Chutneys known as eromba or iromba are also made with chillies, and are served with most dishes.

In Northeast India, vegetarian and non-vegetarian dishes are made with less oil and fewer spices, but they almost always add green or red chillies to their recipes.

It is said that the women of the Northeast own and run the kitchen. It is a woman's domain, where food is served in well-crafted bamboo dishes, which come in all sizes. If not, it is served on banana leaves, steel plates or white China plates.

Serving rice is an art. It is placed in a circle all along the edge of the platter, with the main dish with meat or fish or chicken or vegetables being placed in the centre.

During festivals, the men of the Bnei Menashe Jewish community wear the fringed tallit or tzitzit during prayers at the synagogue. Afterwards, they return home for a sumptuous meal with family and friends. There is no rabbi in Manipur, so an elder of the community, known as a hazzan, leads the prayers. They have a mohel for the circumcision of a male child. As there is no shohet in Manipur, they have learnt to make animals kosher for their own families and sometimes some families do so for other Jewish families. Sometimes they make rice beer, but they try to keep away from most alcoholic drinks and abstain from eating pork.

The Bnei Menashe Jews have fish with scales, meat, chicken, vegetables like pumpkin, cabbage, radish, cauliflower, beans, okra, yam, gourd, tomatoes, potatoes, leafy vegetables like mustard, colocasia, spinach or pumpkin leaves, along with fruits like mango, banana, gooseberries, pineapple, dragon fruit, passionfruit and apples.

At the end of a meal, a variety of fruits is served in bowls to maintain the Jewish dietary law. But sometimes they buy dairy-based Indian sweets from shops and eat them with vegetarian dishes.

FESTIVALS AND OCCASIONS

Shabbath

The Bnei Menashe Jews keep the Shabbath with a deep religious feeling. It is considered to be a time of spiritual refreshment, which is a change from the monotonous routine of daily life. On Friday afternoon, for Shabbath, they buy bread from a bakery or make rice pancakes. Shabbath dinner is cooked by Friday noon. Food is cooked in large quantities so that it lasts till Saturday evening.

The dining table is cleaned, covered with a clean sheet, bread is covered with a ceremonial cloth and homemade wine is made with raisins. In the absence of raisin wine, bottled grape juice of an approved brand is often used for Shabbath prayers and for Jewish festivals.

At the synagogue or at home, Shabbath prayers are chanted in Hebrew.

On Friday evening, candles are lit by the woman of the house, prayers are said over bread and raisin wine, and dinner is served. Their staple diet is fish and rice. Thus Shabbath dinner could be fried fish or fish curry or roast chicken or chicken curry with rice.

If possible, most Bnei Menashe Jews stop work on Shabbath, from Friday night to Saturday evening. Sometimes, men who are employed as professionals cannot keep the Shabbath on Saturday but they make it a point to be present for Friday night prayers, either at home or at the synagogue.They do not drive on Shabbath, nor do they buy newspapers or write, yet women do simple household tasks. The Bnei Menashe Jews spend the Shabbath with a feeling of serenity, tranquility and peace.

Rosh Hashanah

The Jewish New Year is celebrated by blowing the shofar, lighting candles and having apples dipped in honey. Fish heads are made for Rosh Hashanah (recipe on page 32).

Yom Kippur

The Bnei Menashe Jews of Manipur fast during Yom Kippur. In the evening, after the shofar is blown at the synagogue, they break the fast with grape juice, return home and have a simple vegetarian meal.

Purim

Festivals like Purim are often celebrated with a community dinner, which is organized in a rented party hall close to the synagogue. The Bnei Menashe Jews make curry-based fish or chicken or meat dishes with rice and jaggery.

Passover

The Bnei Menashe Jews clean their homes, wash their utensils with warm water, discard all leavened food and prepare matzo pancakes with unleavened flour batter before Passover begins. It is usually celebrated at home during the first two days. The Passover table is decorated with candlestands, their best tableware and wine glasses. The story of the Exodus is read out, followed by a sumptuous meal.

Sukkot

The Festival of Tabernacles or the harvest festival is celebrated by making a tent near a synagogue or the premises of a Jewish home, which is decorated with fruits as thanksgiving for a bountiful harvest.

Shavout

This festival is celebrated to rejoice the receiving of the Ten Commandments on Mount Sinai. This festival celebrates the harvest season for two days and the synagogue is decorated with the first fruits of the season.

Simchat Torah

This festival marks the completion of the reading of the Torah. It is celebrated as a happy event with food which is both sweet and savoury.

Hanukkah

This festive occasion is celebrated by lighting candles. Fried foods like lentil or chickpea-flour vada or pakodas or samosas or gram-flour fritters are made and eaten with potato chips, along with doughnuts.

RECIPES

The Bnei Menashe Jews of Manipur mostly make chicken and fish recipes. Chicken is cooked in mustard oil or soya oil with few spices. They use fiery hot green or red chillies in most recipes. Their staple diet is fish and rice. But on some festive occasions, they have pigeon or duck or bovine meat, which is either roasted or made into a soupy curry. Different types of rice are used in their cuisine. They also make soupy vegetables, masoor dal, meat dishes or fish curries, which are served with rice.

Fish Recipes

Fish Heads

This is a different method from the way the Bene Israel Jews prepare fish heads.

Ingredients

Fish heads – 500 grams
Green chillies – 2
Ginger paste – 1 teaspoon
Salt to taste

Method

Wash fish heads. Lightly grease a flat pan, place fish, simmer on a low flame. Flip the fish heads, add salt, finely chopped green chillies, ginger paste and 1 cup water. Cook on a low flame for five to seven minutes till the fish heads are dry and braised.

Fish Curry

Ingredients

Fish slices – 500 grams
Oil – ¼ cup
Mustard seeds – 1 teaspoon
Cumin seeds – ½ teaspoon
Bay leaf – 1
Onion – 1
Ginger-garlic paste – 1 tablespoon
Tomatoes – 2

Red chilli powder – ¼ teaspoon

Turmeric powder – 1 teaspoon

Green chillies – 2

Coriander leaves – 1 tablespoon

Water – 1 glass

Salt to taste

Method

Clean the fish, soak in water, drain and rub with salt. Fry the fish in oil and keep aside.

Prepare onion paste with onion and 1 teaspoon of water in a blender and keep aside.

In the same oil in which fish was fried, add bay leaf, mustard seeds, cumin seeds, onion paste and ginger-garlic paste. Sauté on a low flame and add finely chopped tomatoes, chilli powder, slit green chillies, turmeric powder, fried fish and water and cook on a medium flame for five to seven minutes, till there is a runny gravy. Garnish with coriander leaves and serve hot with rice.

Fish Cooked in Bamboo Hollow

Ingredients

Whole river fish – 1 fish weighing 500 grams

Oil – 1 tablespoon

Turmeric – ½ teaspoon

Tomato – 1

Onion – 1

Salt to taste

A piece of fresh hollow bamboo for steaming fish

Method

Sweetwater fish is used to make this recipe in a medium-sized bamboo hollow, which is washed, cleaned and kept aside.

Wash the fish, rub with salt and oil, along with a mixture of finely chopped onions, grated ginger and diced green chillies. Gently place the fish in the bamboo hollow and seal with banana leaves or aluminium foil. Cook on a charcoal fire for thirty minutes, rotating slowly on all sides till the fish is tender. Before serving, remove the seal from the bamboo hollow with a thin spatula and place the fish on a serving plate. Cut into portions and serve with rice and gravy-based dishes.

Variation: If bamboo hollow is not available, the fish can be wrapped in cooking foil with the above-mentioned ingredients and baked in a preheated oven for twenty minutes. Sometimes, this recipe is also made with boneless chicken or mutton steaks, which can also be barbecued on a charcoal fire or baked in a preheated oven.

Chicken Recipes

Chicken Curry

This recipe is made with country chicken.

Ingredients

    Chicken – 500 grams
    Ginger – 1 ½ inches
    Rice – ½ cup
    Oil – ¼ cup
    Water as needed
    Salt to taste

Method

Clean, wash and cut chicken into small pieces. Clean and wash the rice and soak in water.

Heat oil in a pan, add chicken pieces and sauté till they are golden brown. Add water to the pan, along with finely chopped ginger and salt. Cover with a lid and cook the chicken till almost done. Remove the lid and add rice to thicken the gravy. Cook on a low flame till done and serve as a one-dish meal.

Chicken Stew

Ingredients

Chicken pieces – 500 grams
Rice – 1 cup
Ginger – 1 ½ inches
Green chillies – 2
Water – 3 glasses
Salt to taste

Method

Clean chicken pieces, soak in a vessel of water, wash, drain and keep aside. Soak rice in another bowl of water, wash, drain and keep aside.

In a heavy casserole, add water and boil on high flame. Add rice, chicken pieces, salt, finely chopped ginger and green chillies. Stir and cook on a low flame for twenty-five minutes till the gravy thickens, rice is cooked and chicken is tender.

Meat Recipes

Mutton Curry

Ingredients

Mutton – 500 grams
Oil – 2 tablespoons
Turmeric powder – ¼ teaspoon
Potatoes – 2
Unripe papaya – 500 grams
Black cardamom pods – 3
Cinnamon – 3-inch stick

Marinade

Onions – 2
Ginger-garlic paste – 2 tablespoons
Black pepper powder – 1 tablespoon
Cumin-coriander powder – 1 tablespoon
Water as specified
Salt to taste

Method

Wash mutton pieces. Process chopped onions, salt, ginger-garlic paste, powdered black pepper, cumin, coriander, cardamom seeds, crushed cinnamon stick with 1 tablespoon water and make a paste. Add the paste to mutton pieces and marinate for thirty minutes.

Peel potatoes and papaya, and wash and cut into slices.

In a casserole, heat oil, add marinated mutton, potatoes and papaya. Add 2 glasses of water, mix well, cover with lid and cook on a medium flame for thirty-five to forty-five minutes. Remove from flame and serve hot with rice.

Fried Meat Strips

Ingredients

 Meat – 500 grams
 Ginger-garlic paste – 1 tablespoon
 Oil for frying
 Salt to taste

Method

Wash the meat, pat dry, marinate in salt and ginger-garlic paste, place in a vessel and cover with a lid. Refrigerate for three hours.

 Heat oil in a heavy kadhai, and fry meat strips till golden brown. Serve with rice or a gravy-based dish. They are also served with fried potato wedges.

Vegetarian Recipes

Elephant Apple or Otenga

Otenga is pronounced as 'ou-tenga'. It is green from the outside and has a white, hard and sour core. The sour taste remains even when the apple is marinated in salt for an hour, boiled in water and drained. These large-sized elephant apples have a tough skin.

Ingredients

 Elephant apple – 300 grams
 Oil – 2 tablespoons
 Turmeric – 1 teaspoon
 Green chillies – 4
 Dry whole chillies – 2

Cumin seeds powder – ¼ teaspoon
Fennel seeds powder – ¼ teaspoon
Nigella seeds – ¼ teaspoon
Fenugreek powder – ¼ teaspoon
Mustard seed paste – 1 tablespoon
Jaggery – 2 tablespoons
Water – 5 glasses
Salt to taste

Method

Cut elephant apple into two halves, peel, separate the petals and further cut into 2-inch pieces. Soak in a bowl of salt water for one hour to remove its tart taste, then drain the water and wash pieces under running water.

In a vessel, boil 3 ½ glasses of water over medium heat, add salt, turmeric and the elephant apple pieces. Cook till tender, drain and keep aside.

In a kadhai, heat oil and temper cumin seeds, fennel seeds, fenugreek seeds, nigella seeds, whole red chillies, slit green chillies and powdered cumin. Add mustard-seed paste, grated jaggery, salt, elephant-apple petals and 1 ½ glasses of water. Cover kadhai with a lid, cook on a medium flame for about fifteen to twenty minutes, till the elephant apple petals cook in a thin gravy. Serve with rice.

Fried Pumpkin

Ingredients

Oil – 1 tablespoon
Pumpkin – 200 grams
Onion – 1

Red chilli powder – 1 teaspoon

Turmeric powder – ½ teaspoon

Salt

Method

Peel, wash and cube pumpkin and keep aside. Heat oil in a vessel and brown sliced onion. Add pumpkin pieces with red chilli powder, turmeric powder and salt. Cooked on a low flame for fifteen minutes till soft. Serve with gravy-based dishes and rice.

Bamboo Shoots with Green Chillies

Ingredients

Bamboo shoots – 500 grams

Green chillies – 50 grams

Water – 5 glasses

Salt to taste

Method

Trim the fibrous outer layers of bamboo shoots, peel the excess leaves, reserve tender leaves and discard one inch of the root as it has a bitter taste. Cut the tender bamboo shoots into two-inch pieces, clean and wash in water.

In a deep vessel, boil water with salt, add bamboo shoots and cook on a high flame for twenty minutes.

In another pan, boil water and add green chillies. Cook for five minutes, remove pan from stove, drain and discard water. Add salt and grind the chillies in a mortar with pestle or process in a blender to make a smooth paste. Cover the bamboo shoots with chilli paste, mix and serve as an accompaniment to most meals.

Variation: You can use red chillies instead of green.

Bamboo Shoots

Vegetable Stew

Ingredients

Red pumpkin leaves – 100 grams

French beans – 12

Medium-sized brinjals – 3

Bamboo shoots – 1 cup

Bhindi or okra – 4

Green chillies – 2

Basil leaves – few

Rice – ½ tablespoon

Salt to taste

Method

Wash tender pumpkin leaves, de-vein, shred. Trim beans, cube brinjals and keep all of them aside on a platter. Clean and wash bamboo shoots as given on page 158 and chop into three-inch pieces. Cut bhindi into small pieces.

In a vessel, boil 1 glass water on a medium flame. Add salt, vegetables, green chillies, rice and basil leaves and stir. Simmer on a low flame for thirty minutes till vegetables are cooked in a soupy stew. Serve hot with rice.

Optional: You can add colocasia and spinach leaves.

Mixed Vegetables

Ingredients

Mustard leaves – 1 cup
Beans – ½ cup
Potato – 1 large
Tomatoes – 3
Green chillies – 4
Garlic – 1 teaspoon
Ginger – 1 tablespoon
Basil leaves – 5
Water – 4 glasses
Salt to taste

Method

Boil water in a vessel, then add shredded mustard leaves, chopped beans, sliced potatoes, cubed tomatoes, salt, slit green chillies, crushed garlic and diced ginger. Cook till potatoes and beans are tender, then garnish with basil leaves and serve hot with rice.

Masala Mixed Vegetables

Ingredients

Pumpkin – ½ cup chopped pieces
Onion – 1 large
Brinjals – 2

Beans – 150 gms
Tomatoes – 3
Red chilli powder – 2 teaspoons
Turmeric powder – ½ teaspoon
Oil – ½ cup
Salt to taste

Method

Heat oil in a pan and brown sliced onions. Add pumpkin pieces along with chopped brinjal, diced beans, cubed tomatoes, red chilli powder, turmeric powder and salt. Stir-fry the mixture till the pumpkin and beans are tender and cooked. Serve with gravy-based vegetables or meat, along with rice.

Note: Sprinkle 1 tablespoon water over the dish when it is half done.

Mustard Leaves in Gravy

Ingredients

Mustard leaves – 1 cup
Green chillies – 3
Tomatoes – 2
Ginger-garlic paste – 1 tablespoon
Mustard oil – ¼ cup
Salt to taste

Method

Wash and shred mustard leaves and keep aside. Heat mustard oil in another vessel and temper chopped green chillies. Add mustard leaves to the chillies along with ginger-garlic paste, salt, chopped tomatoes and water. Cook for fifteen minutes and serve hot with rice.

Soya Beans

Ingredients

> Dried soya beans – 1 cup
> Shredded mustard leaves – 1 cup
> Ginger-garlic paste – 1 tablespoon
> Tomato – 1
> Basil leaves – 5
> Water – 1 litre
> Basil leaves
> Salt to taste

Method

Soak soya beans in a vessel of water for ten hours, covered with a lid. The next day, drain them and pressure-cook in 1 ½ glasses of water for forty minutes till soft. When cool, open the cooker and add salt with shredded mustard leaves, ginger-garlic paste and chopped tomatoes. Mix, stir and cook on a low flame for ten minutes. Garnish with chopped basil leaves and serve with rice.

Potato Curry

Ingredients

> Potatoes – 4 large
> Mustard seeds – ¼ teaspoon
> Cumin seeds – ¼ teaspoon

Red chilli powder – 2 teaspoons
Turmeric powder – ½ teaspoon
Cumin powder – 1 teaspoon
Big tomatoes – 2
Coriander leaves – 2 tablespoons
Salt to taste

Method

Peel and cube potatoes, then boil till soft and keep aside.

Heat oil in a kadhai and temper mustard seeds or cumin seeds. Add cubed potatoes and mix with red chilli powder, turmeric powder, cumin powder and salt. Lightly sauté the potatoes, then add pureed tomatoes. Stir, then cook the dish for a few minutes. Garnish with chopped coriander leaves and serve hot with puris, bread or rice.

Chutneys

Eromba

Ingredients

Whole red chillies – 5
Potatoes – 5
Cabbage/Lettuce - 1 medium
Chives – ¼ cup
Basil leaves – 5
Salt to taste

Method

Boil whole red chillies in a pan of water with salt, peeled and cubed potatoes, chives and shredded leafy vegetables such as cabbage and lettuce. Cook till the sauce thickens and garnish with basil leaves. This chutney is served with gravy-based dishes and rice.

Optional: When in season, chopped fresh beans, slivers of carrot and other vegetables can be added to this chutney.

Variation: This chutney can also be made with peeled and cubed potatoes, fermented bamboo shoots, fermented fish, red chillies and finely chopped garlic. It is garnished with finely chopped coriander leaves.

Bamboo and Green Chilli Chutney

Ingredients

    Tender bamboo shoots – 1 cup
    Green chillies – 3
    Water – 5 glasses
    Salt to taste

Method

Boil green chillies in a pan of water with salt. Drain, pat dry and process in a mixer. Prepare bamboo shoots as given on page 158. In the same water, boil cleaned and washed bamboo shoots for twenty minutes till cooked, drain and keep aside on another plate. Mix the chilli chutney in the bamboo shoots and serve as a one-dish meal or with gravy-based dishes.

Soups

Mustard Leaf Soup

Ingredients

Mustard leaves – 500 grams
Water – 3 cups
Salt to taste

Method

Boil water in a vessel over a medium flame. Add shredded mustard leaves and salt. Cover the vessel with a lid and cook the soup for ten minutes. Mash cooked mustard leaves till soup thickens and serve hot in soup bowls.

Vegetable Soup

Ingredients

Cabbage – 1 cup
Trimmed beans – 1cup
Mustard leaves – ½cup
White pumpkin – ½ cup
Red pumpkin – ½ cup
Lauki or bottle gourd – ½ cup
Zucchini – ½ cup
Green chillies – 4
Basil leaves – few
Coriander leaves – 2 tablespoons
Salt to taste

Method

In a vessel, boil water over a medium flame. Add salt, finely chopped cabbage, trimmed beans, shredded mustard leaves, peeled and cubed pieces of white pumpkin, red pumpkin, bottle gourd, zucchini and slit green chillies. Cook on a medium flame for thirty minutes till the vegetables soften, garnish with finely chopped coriander leaves and basil. Serve hot in soup bowls.

Variation: This recipe can be made with fresh green beans, shredded colocasia leaves, peeled and cubed bottle gourd and slivers of carrots too.

Rice Recipes

Sticky Rice

Ingredients

Sticky rice – 1 cup
Banana leaf – 1

Method

Soak rice in water for four hours, drain and keep aside.

Cut banana leaf into squares, wash, wipe, passed over a live flame to make it pliable and keep aside. Put a ladle-full of rice in the centre of the leaf, fold into a tight packet or tie with cotton strings, place in a steamer for thirty minutes till the rice is soft and cooked. Remove rice packets from the steamer, cool, unwrap and serve with gravy-based dishes.

Rice Cooked in Bamboo Hollow

Ingredients

    Flat sticky rice – 2 cups
    Bamboo hollow – 1
    Banana leaf – 1
    Oil – 1 teaspoon
    Salt to taste
    Water for soaking rice and as specified

Method

Soak rice in water for four to five hours; drain, mix with salt and
¼ cup water. Grind on a stone mortar with a pestle or process in
a mixer. Wash a medium-size bamboo hollow, dry and keep aside.
Cut banana leaf into rectangular pieces, wash, wipe and pass over
a live flame to make it pliable. Roll part of the rice mixture into a
cylindrical shape, pack into the leaf as detailed in the previous recipe
and place in the bamboo hollow. Do the same with the rest of the
rice mixture. Seal with shredded banana leaves or cooking foil. Place
on a charcoal fire or in a preheated oven for twenty-five minutes till
the rice is cooked. When cool, carefully remove it from the bamboo
hollow with a thin spatula and place on a platter. Unwrap from the
banana leaf and serve with gravy-based dishes or as a one-dish meal
with chutneys.

Variation: If bamboo is not available, cooking foil can be used
to make this recipe.

Potato Rolls

Ingredients

Potatoes – 6
Red chilli powder – 2 teaspoon
Cumin powder – 1 ½ teaspoon
Gram flour or besan – 1 cup
Oil for frying
Water as required
Salt to taste

Method

Boil potatoes and mash them. Mix the mash with red chilli powder, cumin and salt. Shape into medium-sized egg-shaped balls and dip in a batter of gram flour.

Heat oil in a kadhai and deep-fry the potato rolls till golden brown. Serve hot as a snack with tea or drinks.

Pancakes

The Bnei Menashe Jews often have a breakfast of pancakes with honey.

Ingredients

Rice powder or black rice powder – 4 cups
Water – as required
Refined flour – 1 cup
Banana leaves – 8

Method

Make a dough out of rice powder and water. Roll into small balls and flatten into squares on a board with a rolling pin. Cut banana leaves into squares, place a rice powder square on each leaf and fold into a packet. Steam all the packets till done and serve hot or cold.

Pancakes can also be made with black rice. Soak the black rice overnight, grind on a stone mortar with a pestle or process in a mixer into a smooth paste. Remove onto a platter and make into a dough by mixing with refined flour and water. Make small balls out of the dough, flatten into chapattis on a rolling board, then roast on a griddle and flip so that both sides are cooked till they are crisp.

Note: For Hanukkah and Sukkot, Bnei Menashe Jews have doughnuts with a jam topping and pancakes with honey.

Desserts

Jaggery Sweets

Ingredients

Puffed rice – 250 grams
Jaggery – 750 grams
Peanuts (for the variation) – 100 grams

Method

Heat puffed rice and jaggery together in a pan, stirring continuously, till the jaggery melts and the mixture starts sticking to the pan. Remove from the stove. When cool, shape this mixture into small balls and place on a platter and serve. This can be stored in a container for later consumption as well.

Variation: Heat finely chopped jaggery in a pan with water and stir continuously so that the jaggery does not burn. When the mixture starts sticking to the base, add peanuts and stir continuously. Then pour the mixture into a baking tray, cool, cut into squares and serve or store in a container. This recipe can also be made with sesame seeds.

Chak-hao or Black Rice Pudding

Black rice is grown in Northeast India and used to make rice pudding. It has a medium nutty grain, purple colour and a sweet flavour. Black rice or purple rice pudding, known as chak-hao, takes forty-five minutes to one hour to cook.

Ingredients

Black rice – ½ cup
Coconut milk – 1 litre
Sugar – ¾ cup
Cardamom powder – 1 teaspoon
Nutmeg powder – ¼ teaspoon
Cashew nuts – 1 tablespoon
Almonds – 1 tablespoon
Grated coconut – ¼ cup
Water – 3 glasses

Method

Soak rice in warm water for five hours or overnight, drain, partially cook in a pan or pressure-cook with 1 cup of water.

In a heavy-bottomed pan, mix rice with coconut milk and cook on a medium flame for forty-five minutes to one hour, stirring continuously, till rice is tender. Add sugar, cardamom powder, grated nutmeg and simmer on a low flame till the rice pudding has a soft, smooth, creamy consistency. Garnish with finely chopped nuts and shredded coconut.

Note: Sometimes, cakes are also made with powdered black rice.

Doughnuts

Ingredients

> Refined flour – 1 cup
> Yeast – ½ tablespoon
> Milk – ½ cup milk
> Sugar – 3 tablespoons

Method

Make a dough out of refined flour, yeast, milk and sugar and keep aside in a covered vessel for an hour. Then cut the dough into balls, roll out each ball on a board with a rolling pin into thick roundels and keep aside. Cut a hole with a cookie-cutter in the centre of each roundel.

Heat oil in a kadhai, and deep-fry the doughnuts. Remove onto a grease-proof paper and serve with a dusting of powdered sugar or decorate with a topping of jam or jelly. To maintain the dietary law, these doughnuts are served with vegetarian food.

8

The Bnei Menashe Jews of Mizoram

A young journalist passing through Ahmedabad once came to meet me. He had just been to Mizoram and described the beautiful landscape of northeast India in poetic terms. He told me about how a cloud had floated through the window into his hotel room.

Hence, I was looking forward to going to Mizoram, which was part of my project to study the cuisine of the Bnei Menashe Jews who live there. Much before I went, whenever I saw books or television shows on Mizoram, I would be fascinated by their textiles, shawls and bamboo artifacts. I had also seen their bamboo dance at folk-dance festivals.

Yonathan Lallawmsanga, a prominent Jew of Mizoram, helped me with the process to enter the state. He also sent me the address of the Beit Knesset Synagogue in Aizawl.

When I landed at the airport with its tabletop runway, I saw tall mountain tops amidst floating clouds, which descended into the lush green valleys. I stopped at the military checkpost, where I filled the forms and gave the necessary papers for my permit to stay in Mizoram.

My taxi from the airport drove through winding roads spiralling and ascending the mountain range, overlooking hills and valleys. The landscape was breathtakingly beautiful – mountains, valleys, tall trees, bamboo thickets, plantain groves, flowering trees and orchards. Ferns, creepers, orchids and other flowers covered the mountain slopes. As the car passed by a waterfall, I saw people bathing or washing clothes in the water. On the roadside along the route, there were flocks of country chicken, herds of goats and vendors selling packets of fresh bamboo shoot.

When I reached Aizawl, I saw houses on stilts and double-storeyed houses with slanting roofs, topped with water storage tanks painted in different colours, which were built on the mountain slopes. Most houses and streets were interconnected with uneven staircases. The street leading to my hotel was lined with grocery shops, bakeries, bamboo artifacts and vegetable shops. The mountains and valleys appeared to be far away from these steep streets, which were winding upwards with sharp turns.

It was Friday evening, the Shabbath, and not yet 7 p.m., so I thought I had time to find the synagogue. Quickly, I took a taxi. It was getting dark, but after many twists and turns on the winding roads, the taxi driver stopped from across the synagogue. There were lights on the third floor of the building. When I heard the beautiful chants of Shabbath prayers, I felt elated. It was an old four-storeyed building, which had a small plaque with a Star of David that read: Beit Knesset Synagogue.

I climbed the staircase and reached a long hall with a balcony, where prayers were being held. The men were on the left side of the hall, the women on the right, and a transparent gossamer curtain with embroidered patterns separated the women's section from the men's. There was a small platform, or Teva, behind which there was an Ark with a silk curtain. The hazzan, dressed in a black suit and hat, was standing on the Teva and leading the prayers. I joined the women's congregation. The curtain was raised and a young Israeli man wearing a kippa gave a sermon in English about Moses and the Ten Commandments, while the hazzan translated the same into Mizo. I looked into the prayer book of the lady standing next to me and saw that the Mizo words were spelled out in English. I was told that this is how the Mizo language is written. Soon after, the curtain was lowered with the last chant of the Shabbath prayers.

The women affectionately wished me Shabbath-shalom and we shook hands. I looked around and noticed that the men were in casuals with kippas pinned on their heads, while the women were beautifully dressed in skirts, sarongs or fitted sheathes worn with jackets, and their heads were covered with colourful scarves or tassled shawls. Most of the women had long hair, which flowed over their shoulders or had been tied in a topknot. They were all dressed up for Shabbath. Some women were carrying their babies, who were tied with shawls on their backs.

After Shabbath services, I met the hazzan, introduced myself and told him about the project. He informed me, 'Nobody works on

Shabbath, but you can go down to the first floor for the Shabbath Kiddush.'

This was where Shalom, an elderly lady who was a betel-nut vendor, lived. She welcomed me into her one-room flat and introduced her family. On a small table, there were Shabbath candles and a Kiddush glass filled with raisin wine and fruit buns for the Hamotzi prayers, which were kept on a plate and covered with a ceremonial cloth. Her son said the prayers and the women brought soup plates filled with broth made with brinjals and potatoes and topped with fermented fish, a plate of boiled pumpkin pieces and a huge vessel of white sticky rice. I could not stay for dinner, but I was told that no Jewish person would give me information about Bnei Menashe Jewish food on Saturday, the Shabbath.

I was disappointed. So, I spent Saturday in the marketplace, where I found traditional textile shops and bamboo artifacts. That evening, I spent a long time at the Khatla food market, held on a long winding street, where innumerable vendors were sitting in rows with their wares, including fruits and vegetables. This street extended to the meat market, where chicken and fish were available. I also saw ducks and geese strutting around but was not sure if they were for sale. Live chicken were sold in bamboo-strip packets, while some fruit and vegetables were wrapped in large leaves. There were mounds of pineapples, apples, oranges, sweet lime, out-of-season mangoes, berries, black and green grapes, guava, papaya, pomegranate, dragon fruit, passionfruit and even coconut, both tender and dry. Cut fruit was also sold in plates, neatly covered with cling-film.

Dragonfruit

Next to these, there were pumpkins of all sizes – both yellow and white – bottle-gourd, brinjals, chillies of all sizes, shapes and colour including fiery hot raja chillies and bhut jolokia chillies, many varieties of mushrooms, leafy vegetables like spinach, mustard, colocasia, along with okra, cabbage, cauliflower, beans in short and long pods, carrots, ridge gourd, radish, cucumber, tomatoes, coriander leaves, basil leaves, huge tangy lemons and other vegetables. There was also lots of fresh ginger, galangal, turmeric, colacasia roots and maize. Onions were sold along with potatoes and trays of eggs were stacked over each other.

Women vendors were selling packaged Mizo tea, powdered spices, fermented soya beans or fermented fish or meat in huge vessels along with barbecued meat.

Sealed clay pots were also kept near some food stalls, as these are traditionally used to ferment a variety of foods that are used in Mizo cuisine.

On Sunday, I met Yonathan and his mother Tamar Lalhmachhuani for lunch. Tamar told us about their family. Her daughter had emigrated to Israel with her children and eventually Yonathan and Tamar would follow her. They spent the afternoon with me and patiently answered my questions. When they left, they reassured me about sending me as many details as possible about Bnei Menashe cuisine; and they did. I was happy that my trip to Aizawl was worthwhile. Not only was I able to explore the food markets to see the ingredients available to the Bnei Menashe Jews of Mizoram, I also got to meet them and experience a Shabbath meal.

The Bnei Menashe Jews in Mizoram follow much the same rituals as their kin in Manipur. Community dinners are not held at a prayer hall or synagogue, but sometimes the Jews of Mizoram organize dinners at party halls or rooms next to the synagogue of the Shavei Israel Centre in Aizawl. They believe that a family must eat together for unity and solidarity.

They celebrate festivals with fish, rice, dal and potatoes. They have rice almost every day with every meal. They have a preference for sunflower oil in their cuisine.

They also follow the strict dietary laws of kosher. With limited resources, they observe and follow Jewish rites, rituals and traditions. In the absence of a shohet in Mizoram, most Jewish families have learnt to prepare meat in a kosher way, according to the Jewish dietary law.

They keep separate dishes for vegetarian and non-vegetarian dishes. It is important to mention that their meals end with bowls of fresh fruit or chopped betel nut rolled in betel leaves, which are available in marketplaces, stalls, shops and grocery stores all over Mizoram. Sometimes, they serve bowls of fresh fruit or cubed jaggery with meat dishes. They make sweets with dairy products when they have vegetarian meals. Tea is made using chopped jaggery as a sweetener.

In Mizoram, when any leafy vegetable is shredded and boiled in a vessel along with ginger, slit green chillies and salt, it is known as Bai, and is a traditional favourite of their cuisine. And when food is fried, it is known as Kan.

Bai and Kan apply to both vegetarian and non-vegetarian dishes like fish, meat and chicken, which are cut into big pieces. On some festive occasions, they have pigeon or duck or bovine meat, which are either roasted or made into a soupy curry. Their method of cooking retains the original flavours of food with minimum spices and other ingredients.

Some Mizo homes have kitchen gardens where they grow their own chillies, turmeric and ginger, which they use when necessary. Often, ginger is cleaned, washed, scraped, cut into small pieces, marinated in salt, kept in a bowl on the side and served with some dishes. Their staple diet is fish and rice. Permitted meats are rubbed with salt, washed in water and cooked. Most homes have a brick oven, which resembles a furnace, where fish or cubed meat is cooked on skewers and served with beans. Packaged fermented meat is also available in shops and is used by the Bnei Menashe Jews. The kitchen is almost always stocked with bananas and a a variety of leafy vegetables, like colocasia and mustard. Fish, meat and soya beans are also part of a Mizo meal. Festive events are often observed as a holiday by the Jewish community and they rejoice by drinking bowls of rice beer with family and friends. A platter or thali or banana leaf is often prepared with cooked vegetables and meat dishes, along with dal, rice and chutneys.

FESTIVALS AND OCCASIONS

Shabbath

The Bnei Menashe Jews observe Shabbath as a form of spiritual refreshment and a change from the monotonous routine of daily life, as they believe in rest days and holy days. They buy bread from a bakery on Friday afternoon for Shabbath services. Some Jewish women have learnt to bake challah bread with refined flour. Sometimes, challah bread is made by the synagogue committee and sold to Jewish families to raise funds for community activities. When challah bread is not available, white bread or sweet buns are bought from local bakeries. For Shabbath dinner and other Jewish festivals, gravy-based dishes with chicken or fish or meat are made and served with rice. Homemade wine for Kiddush prayers is also prepared. Grapes or raisins are cleaned, washed, boiled and filtered to make Shabbath wine.

Passover

The Bnei Menashe Jews celebrate Passover on the first and second evening of the festival. For the Jews of Northeast India, it is celebrated at home. Before Passover begins, Jewish women clean their homes and discard all leavened foods, like bread, which is not served during these days. Matzo chapattis are made with unleavened refined-flour dough. Sometimes, the Bnei Menashe Jews of Mizoram receive matzo packets from Israel, which are placed on Passover platters. Extra matzo bread is given to those present for the Seder. The Passover table is covered with a clean tablecloth and decorated with flowers, candles, plates and wine glasses. A platter is prepared for the Passover Seder with matzo chapattis, dates, a bowl of salt water, bitter herbs, the roasted leg of a chicken and boiled eggs, which are symbolic of life. The story of the Exodus from Egypt is read by an elder or the hazzan of the synagogue.

Rosh Hashanah

The Jewish New Year is celebrated by blowing the shofar at the synagogue, lighting candles and having sliced apples dipped in honey. For the New Year, the Bnei Menashe Jews also have pomegranate seeds, almonds, sautéed fish heads, stir-fried pumpkin slices, fried onion roots and a gravy-based dish of chicken or fish or meat, which is served with rice.

A similar meal is made for Shabbath and other Jewish festivals. But fish heads are made specially for the New Year, along with homemade wine or bottled grape juice of an approved brand bought from the market.

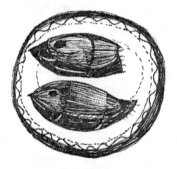

Fish Heads

Yom Kippur

The Bnei Menashe Jews fast on the Day of Atonement. They break the fast with homemade grape-juice wine, snacks, fritters and simple vegetarian dishes, which are served with rice.

Simchat Torah

During Simchat Torah, the Bnei Menashe Jews of Mizoram gather at a community hall near the synagogue, where they prepare a variety of gravy-based dishes with chicken or meat or fish, along with rice. This festival is celebrated with fun and gaiety.

Hanukkah

This festival is celebrated by lighting candles. The Bnei Menashe Jews have biscuits, cakes and fritters. They also make gravy-based dishes of fish or chicken or meat, which are served with fried fish or fermented fish and rice. Grape-juice wine is made with raisins, which is filtered, bottled and served in glasses.

Rice wine is made by the Bnei Menashe Jews of Mizoram for festive occasions.

RECIPES

Vegetable Soup

Ingredients

    Brinjals – 3
    Pumpkin leaves – 2 cups
    Bamboo shoots – 1 cup
    Green chillies – 3
    Water – 5 glasses

Method

Boil water in a vessel. Add chopped brinjals, deveined pumpkin leaves and salt. Add bamboo shoots prepared as described on page 158. Cook for twenty-five minutes and serve hot in soup bowls.

Variation: You can also add cabbage leaves, mustard leaves and garnish with a few basil leaves.

Fish Recipes

Fish with Mustard Leaves

Ingredients

Mustard leaves – 300 grams
Green chillies – 3
Water – 3 glasses
Garlic (optional) – 2 cloves
Salt to taste

Method

Cut a whole fish into medium-sized pieces, clean, wash and keep aside. Boil water in a vessel and add fish pieces with slit green chillies, salt and shredded mustard leaves. Cook till the water reduces and serve with rice.

Variation: Freshly caught fish can also be boiled with crushed garlic, slit green chillies, salt, shredded mustard leaves and served with rice.

Boiled Fish

This is a light gravy made with river fish, like rohu.

Ingredients

Fish – 1 whole
Water – 2 cups
Salt to taste

Method

Wash and clean fish, marinate with salt and keep aside. Boil water in a pan and place the fish carefully in the boiling water. Cook till tender, then sprinkle with salt and served with rice. The fish stock is retained and served in soup bowls.

Fried Fish

Recipe given on page 152

Bamboo-cooked Fish

Recipe given on page 152

Chicken Recipes

Braised Chicken

Ingredients

Chicken – 500 grams
Garlic – 6 cloves
Water – 6 glasses
Rice flour – 2 tablespoons
Salt to taste

Method

Clean and wash a whole chicken and keep aside. In a heavy-bottomed vessel, boil water on a low flame after adding crushed garlic and salt. As the water boils, add chicken and cook for twenty-five minutes, add rice-flour slurry to the stock and cook on a high flame for ten more minutes. When water reduces and the chicken is done, remove it onto a board, cut into pieces, return to the vessel, cook again on a high flame for a few minutes and serve with rice.

Note: Boiled chicken and whole chicken with broth are also made with the above-mentioned recipe.

Variation: Heat oil in a vessel and brown sliced onions. Add chicken pieces, crushed garlic, diced green chillies, turmeric powder and salt, along with water. Cook till done and serve with rice.

Chicken Strips

Ingredients

Boneless chicken – 500 grams

Soya sauce – 2 tablespoons

Chilli sauce – 2 tablespoons

Onions – 2

Ginger – 2 tablespoons

Garlic – 1 teaspoon

Capsicum – 1 large

Green chillies – 3

Tomatoes – 2

Parkia beans – 1 teaspoon

Black pepper powder – 1 teaspoon

Salt to taste

Method

Cut boneless pieces of chicken into strips. Wash, pat dry, then marinate in soya sauce and red chilli sauce for an hour.

Heat oil in a kadhai and fry sliced onions till transparent. Then sauté finely diced ginger, garlic, chopped capsicum, sliced green chillies, cubed tomatoes, parkia beans, black pepper powder and salt. Mix chicken strips with the above-mentioned ingredients and cook on a low flame till done. Serve as a snack with rice beer.

Chicken Pulao

Ingredients

Basmati rice – 1 ½ cups

Chicken pieces – 500 grams

Bay leaf – 1

Black cardamom – 2

Raja chillies or dry red chillies – 2

Black pepper powder – 1 teaspoon

Celery – 2 stalks

Leeks – 2

Mustard leaves – 7

Rice beer – 2 tablespoons

Parkia beans – 2

Salt to taste

Method

Soak rice in water, wash, drain and keep aside. In a heavy-bottomed vessel, boil chicken pieces with a bay leaf, a few black cardamoms, fiery hot raja chillies or dry red chillies, black pepper powder, chopped celery, chopped leeks, mustard leaves and salt. Cook on a low flame till the chicken is almost done. Add the rice to the chicken and stir and cook on a low flame till done. Drain excess water from the vessel and cook on a low flame for a few more minutes. Then open the lid and pour 2 spoons of beer or wine over the pulao, along with 2 chopped parkia beans, which lend an aromatic flavour to the dish. Cover with a lid and cook for a few more minutes. The aroma of the pulao will fill the house.

Note: The taste of pulao differs when it is cooked with wine or beer.

Variation: A simpler version of pulao can be made with rice and medium-sized pieces of chicken, which are boiled with the rice, finely diced ginger, slit green chillies and salt till done.

Meat Recipes

Meat Curry

This is made on festive occasions.

Ingredients

    Meat – 500 grams
    Onions – 2
    Garlic – 1 tablespoon
    Turmeric powder – 1 teaspoon
    Green chillies – 2
    Oil – 2 tablespoons
    Salt to taste

Method

Cube meat, clean, wash, soak in salt water, wash again and keep aside. Heat oil in a heavy-bottomed vessel and brown sliced onions, along with the meat and crushed garlic. Simmer on a low flame for five minutes. Add water along with turmeric powder, slit green chillies and salt, then stir the dish and cook for thirty-five minutes. Serve with rice.

Meat Fry

Ingredients

 Boneless meat – 500 grams
 Vinegar – ¼ cup
 Lemon juice – 1 tablespoon
 Basil leaves – 6
 Mustard seeds, powdered – 1 teaspoon
 Black pepper powder – 1 teaspoon
 Rice flour – 1 cup
 Cornflour – 1 cup
 Eggs – 2
 Oil for marinating and frying

Method

Wash boneless meat pieces, pat dry, then marinate in a bowl with oil, vinegar, lemon juice, chopped basil leaves, powdered mustard seeds, black pepper and salt.

In another bowl, mix rice flour, cornflour and beaten eggs, whisk into a batter and keep aside.

Coat meat pieces with the above mixture.

Heat oil in a kadhai and fry the meat pieces on a low flame till they are crisp and golden brown. Serve as a one-dish meal with fried potatoes and boiled vegetables.

Meat Strips

Recipe given on page 156.

Vegetarian Recipes

Elephant Apple or Otenga

Recipe given on page 157.

Bamboo Shoot Sauce

Ingredients

> Bamboo shoots – 250 grams
> Mushrooms – 150 gms
> Oil – 1 tablespoon
> Water as needed
> Salt to taste

Method

Clean and wash tender bamboo shoots as per the method given on page 158 and boil with salt in a pan of water till done. Sauté mushrooms and garnish the soupy sauce with them.

Variation: Clean and wash bamboo shoots, blanch and drain. Heat oil in a pan and stir-fry bamboo shoots with two chopped green chillies and salt.

Colocasia Stir-fry

Ingredients

> Colocasia leaves – 500 grams
> Onions – 2

Oil – 1 tablespoon

Salt to taste

Method

Devein colocasia leaves, wash, shred and keep aside. Heat oil in a pan and fry sliced onions. Add colocasia leaves with salt and sauté till tender. Serve with rice.

Pakora or Pakore

Ingredients

Gram flour powder or besan – 1 cup

Red chilli powder – 1 teaspoon

Turmeric powder – 1 teaspoon

Cumin – 1 teaspoon

Coriander powder – 1 teaspoon

Fresh coriander – ¼ cup

Salt to taste

Water

Method

Make a batter of gram flour with red chilli powder, turmeric, coriander, cumin, fresh coriander leaves, salt and water.

Heat oil in a kadhai and drop a spoonful of batter into it. Deep-fry till the pakodas puff up. Remove with a slotted spoon, drain and keep aside on a plate. Repeat this process till the entire batter is used up. Serve pakodas with tea or drinks or make into a pakoda curry as given in the next recipe.

Pakoda Curry

Ingredients

> Chickpeas – 150 grams
> Oil – 2 tablespoons
> Bay leaf – 1
> Turmeric powder – ½ teaspoon
> Red chilli powder – 1teaspoon
> Cumin powder – 1 teaspoon
> Coriander powder – 1 teaspoon
> Ginger paste – 1 teaspoon
> Fresh coriander leaves – 1 tablespoon
> Salt to taste

Method

Soak chickpeas overnight in a vessel of water. Drain in the morning, wash and pressure-cook with three whistles for forty minutes till soft. When cool, mash chickpeas with a ladle and strain excess water through a sieve in another vessel.

Heat oil in a deep-bottomed vessel and temper bay leaf, ginger paste, turmeric powder, cumin powder, coriander leaves and salt. Add excess chickpea water and boil on a low flame till sauce thickens. Add gram flour pakodas (recipe on page 189) to the gravy, along with the remaining chickpeas. Cook for five minutes, garnish with coriander leaves and serve hot with rice.

Chutneys

Green Chilli Chutney

Ingredients

> Green chillies – 250 grams
> Onions – 1
> Garlic – 1 teaspoon
> Bamboo shoots (variation) – 1 cup
> Ginger (variation) – 1 tablespoon
> Salt to taste

Method

Grind green chillies with a mortar and pestle or process in a mixer with onions, garlic and salt. This chutney is served with most meals.

Variation: Boil chillies in a pan of water with salt, remove, drain the water, pat dry, grind in a mortar with a pestle or process in a mixer. Use the excess water used to boil the chillies to boil cleaned bamboo shoots till done. Drained and serve bamboo shoots along with the chilli chutney.

Optional: Green chillies can also be roasted in a pan or on an open fire.

Note: This chutney is also made with dry red chillies.

Egg Chutney

Ingredients

> Eggs – 6
> Ginger paste – 1 teaspoon
> Salt to taste

Method

Hardboiled eggs are used to make this chutney. Peel eggs, mash in a bowl, mix with ginger paste and salt, then serve with gravy-based dishes and rice.

Rice Recipes

The Bnei Menashe Jews of Mizoram also make rice in a bamboo hollow and puffed rice laddoos, just like the Jews of Manipur (see pages 167 and 169 for recipes).

Rice Puris

Ingredients

    Uncooked rice – 1 ½ cups
    Sugar or jaggery – ½ cups
    Oil to fry
    Pinch of salt
    Banana leaves (variation)

Method

Roast or dry rice, then powder in a stone mortar with a pestle or process in a mixer. Mix with sugar or powdered jaggery, then make into a dough with water. Cut the dough into even-sized balls and roll into puris on a board with a rolling pin.

Heat oil in a kadhai and fry the puris. Flip with a slotted spoon so that both halves are cooked evenly, till done. Remove, drain, place on a greaseproof paper and store in a container.

Rice Poories

Variation: Savoury rice cakes can also be made with the same recipe where salt is added to the powdered rice instead of sugar or jaggery.

Raw rice can also be used to make rice cakes. Soak rice in water, drain, dry, roast and powder in a mixer. Mix with powdered jaggery, make into a dough with water and keep aside. Cut banana leaves into squares, clean on both sides, dry and quickly pass over a live flame to make them pliable. Shape the dough into flat balls. Place each ball on a banana leaf square and fold into a packet, tie with cotton string and keep aside. When all the rice balls are packed, steam them till done. When cool, open the packets and serve with tea or rice beer.

Pancakes

Ingredients

    Rice – 2 cups
    Salt to taste
    Warm water as needed

Method

Soak rice overnight in water. The next day, drain, dry, grind on a stone mortar with a pestle or process in a mixer, to make it into a fine powder. Add salt and water and remove into a bowl. Combine rice flour, salt and warm water; knead into a soft dough and divide into small balls. Place each ball on a board, shape like flatbread, then roast on a griddle on a low flame. Flip on both sides till done and serve with honey.

Variation: The pancake dough can also be made with sticky rice, which has to be steamed in a banana leaf as given in the previous recipe.

Acknowledgements

I would like to thank the following:

- The Hadassah Brandeis Research Award, USA, for funding my project.

- Julie Joseph Pingle, who gave me detailed information about the cuisine of the Bene Israel Jews of western India and also cooked some traditional recipes, which I documented. The Bene Israel Jews of Ahmedabad, Gujarat, whom I met at the Magen Abraham Synagogue, for their inputs. The Bene Israel Jews of Mumbai and Alibaug in Raigad district, Maharashtra, for their cooperation.

- Ian Zachariah for giving me detailed information about the cuisine of the Baghdadi Jews of Kolkata.

- Ofera Elias and Elias Joseph Hai for a warm welcome when we met at the Kadavumbagam Synagogue in Kochi, Kerala.

Thanks also to Ofera for introducing me to achappams and giving me information about the cuisine of Cochin Jews of Kerala.

- Mukthipudi Jaya Kumar Jacob (Jaya Kumar) for receiving me at Vijayawada's Gannavaram airport, arranging for transport to reach Machilipatnam and giving me information about the Bene Ephraim Jews of Andhra Pradesh, along with the recipes he had collected from women of the Jewish community, which he translated from Telugu to English. I was touched by his hospitality.

- Lhingneikim Manchong and Akiva Haokip Khailen for their inputs on the cuisine of the Bnei Menashe Jews of Manipur.

- Yonathan Lallawmsanga and his mother Tamar Lalhmachhuani for their inputs on the cuisine of the Bnei Menashe Jews of Mizoram.

- It was a chance meeting with J.C. Haldar and Dalia Ray of Kolkata at the Magen Abraham Synagogue, Ahmedabad, where they told me about challah bread and agar-agar jelly prepared by the Baghdadi Jews. Thanks to them for that.

- Dr Anil Gupta, a pioneer in grassroots innovations and retired faculty, IIM Ahmedabad, for giving me the contact numbers of people in Mizoram. He started the traditional food fair 'Satvik' in Ahmedabad, which helped popularize Jewish cuisine.

- Dwithiya Raghavan for cooking Bene Ephraim Jewish recipes for me, like chicken curry with gongura leaves and coloured rice, when we met in Hyderabad. Earlier, she has cooked recipes from my novels and written about them.

- Dr Shwetal Gadhavi and Shefali Nayan for their support.